Gallé Lamps

Gallé Lamps

Alastair Duncan and Georges de Bartha

ANTIQUE COLLECTORS' CLUB

ISBN 978 1 85149 671 6

British Library Cataloguing-in-Publication Data:
A catalogue record for this book is available from the British Library.

Endpaper: View of the decorating studio, showing a row of glass artisans at their work benches;
behind them editions of acid-etched glassware
Frontispiece: Mould-blown Rhododendron table lamp
Page 6: Chrysanthemum table lamp

Printed in China for
Antique Collectors' Club Ltd., Woodbridge, Suffolk, IP12 4SD

THE ANTIQUE COLLECTORS' CLUB

Formed in 1966, the Antique Collectors' Club is now a world-renowned publisher of top quality books for the collector. It also publishes the only independently-run monthly antiques magazine, *Antique Collecting*, which rose quickly from humble beginnings to a network of worldwide subscribers.

The magazine, whose motto is *For Collectors-By Collectors-About Collecting*, is aimed at collectors interested in widening their knowledge of antiques both by increasing their awareness of quality and by discussion of the factors influencing prices.

Subscription to *Antique Collecting* is open to anyone interested in antiques, and subscribers receive ten issues a year. Well-illustrated articles deal with practical aspects of collecting and provide numerous tips on prices, features of value, investment potential, fakes and forgeries. Offers of related books at special reduced prices are also available only to subscribers.

In response to the enormous demand for information on 'what to pay', ACC introduced in 1968 the famous price guide series. The first title, *The Price Guide to Antique Furniture*, now renamed *British Antique Furniture: Price Guide and Reasons for Values*, is regularly updated and in constant demand. Since those pioneering days, ACC has gone from strength to strength, publishing many of today's standard works of reference on all things antique and collectable, from *Tiaras* to *20th Century Ceramic Designers in Britain*.

Not only has ACC continued to cater strongly for its original audience, it has also branched out to produce excellent titles on many subjects including art reference, architecture, garden design, fashion, and textiles. All ACC's publications are available through bookshops worldwide and a catalogue is available free of charge from the addresses below.

For further information please contact:

www.antiquecollectorsclub.com

Antique Collectors' Club
Sandy Lane, Old Martlesham
Woodbridge, Suffolk IP12 4SD, UK
Tel: 01394 389950 Fax: 01394 389999
Email: info@antique-acc.com
or
ACC Distribution
6 West 18th Street, Suite 4B,
New York, NY 10011, USA
Tel: 212 645 1111
Fax: 212 989 3205
Email: sales@antiquecc.com

CONTENTS

Chapter 1:

GALLÉ'S CRISTALLERIE

Emile Gallé, c. 1890

Top: Detailed view of the lower marquetry panels on the vitrine, depicting operations in the glass workshops at the Cristalleries de Gallé

It is unclear why Gallé was not drawn sooner to lamps as a medium for his art glass. Perhaps the early uncertainty about the commercial dependability of electricity was a sufficient deterrent; the sputtering, feeble yellow glow of the early incandescent filament light bulb was hardly a trustworthy vehicle by which to promote one's work. Whatever the reason, lamps did not form a significant part of Gallé's repertoire in glass until immediately prior to 1900; no mention was made of them in his *Notes to the Juries* of the 1884 and 1889 Expositions and only brief reference to the single example he displayed at the 1892 Salon of La Société Nationale des Beaux-Arts at the Pavillon de Marsan, Paris – described, but not illustrated, in his entry in the Salon catalogue as a *Crépescule* lamp in violet-aubergine tones. Nor was specific mention made in the firm's 1900 catalogue of the selection of lamps included in his display at that year's Exposition Universelle; a few examples were listed but not illustrated. Only in the last few years of his life does it appear that Gallé realised the full aesthetic potential of opalescent glass viewed by transmitted light; his daughter, Thérèse later recounted that the family home, La Garenne, was only electrified in 1902.

Of the relatively few non-commercial examples that have survived from these formative years, none disappoint. His firm's posthumous models, however, if anything, utilised the medium more effectively. Double- and triple-layered cameo table lamps, chandeliers, sconces and night lights – some models with moulded relief definition that were introduced only in the 1920s – utilised the brilliance of electricity with magical effect, highlighting the blended colours within the superimposed layers of translucent glass.

The showroom at the Gallé workshops, post-1900, including a selection of table lamps and a chandelier

Gallé at La Garenne, c1890

The wedding party at the marriage of Gallé's daughter, Thérèse, at La Garenne, the family residence, in 1902. Gallé is in the front row at the top of the steps on the left

The Glassworkers

Formal group photograph of the staff at the Cristallerie Gallé. Gallé is seated, fourth from the right, 1897

In the late 19th century, Alsace-Lorraine was richly endowed in glass tradition; the vast forests of the neighbouring region provided glasshouses with the fuel necessary to heat their furnaces. Beyond Nancy, the ancestral seat of power, the industry had spread south-east to Luneville, north to Longwy and Metz, and north-east to Meisenthal, the last-mentioned annexed in 1871 by Germany following the Franco-Prussian war. Also nearby, in the Moselle region, was St. Louis, celebrated for its millefiore paperweights.

An army of artisans, their skills interchangeable, serviced the numerous glasshouses. Apprenticeship in one was often followed by a fresh start elsewhere. Armed with his new qualifications, a journeyman artisan might well effect a brighter career where his earlier, perhaps uncelebrated, training was unknown. There was, therefore, a lively traffic between glasshouses, one which accelerated as a firm's economic fortunes rose and fell from year to year in the battle for commissions. It was from this itinerant labour force that Gallé first had to search for workers. Soon his rapid accomplishments and reputation for even-handedness drew the province's finest directly to the gates of 39 avenue de la Garenne. From this elite band, the team was picked that would complete experiments, which, in turn, propelled Gallé toward new discoveries. The number of employees quickly swelled as early successes brought increased sales. In 1883, Roger Marx indicated in the *Nancy Artiste* the speed at which the glassworks was expanding, writing that Gallé had 'under his direction a pleiad of artists. Prouvé made his first essay there, Uriot and Hestaux work there, the young sculptor Jacquot has recently joined; they find themselves in a milieu which greatly contributes to the development of the artistic fibre which they all possess. And I ask myself if one should envy Gallé for employing such artists or if it is not better to congratulate these youngsters for having such a master as their leader.'

By 1889, the number of glass artisans was listed at 300. Included under the broad heading of *verriers* were designers, enamellers, engravers, etchers, polishers, chemists and blowers, all supported by teams of apprentices and unskilled aides; stock-takers, packers and shippers completed the count.

Part of Gallé's genius lay in his ability to share the credit with his collaborators. Though always effectively in command – designing or overseeing the multiplicity of projects underway simultaneously within the plant – he realised that individual ambitions had to be catered to, that egos had continually to be massaged. He managed this with more self-confidence than many. Tiffany, for example, tried to keep the names of his designers and glass artists a virtual secret for fifty years, leading several top window designers to branch out on their own.

Understandably, the names of Gallé's earliest employees were not as well documented as those of the heady years 1900-1904, when the international art community turned its full gaze on every facet of his life and work. The earliest collaborator was, of course, Victor Prouvé, whose ubiquitous talents were soon drawn upon freely by all of Nancy's art community. In the 1880s came Louis Hestaux (1858-1919), Uriot (1852-?), and Marcelin Daigueperce (?-1896). Hestaux, in particular, appears from the start to have been accorded a special place, and was credited with numerous works in glass and furniture throughout a long and distinguished employment. Most of the glass artists who helped in Gallé's *tours de force* at the turn-of-the-century joined the firm in the early-to-mid-1890s, many in 1894 when the new glassworks opened. These included Albert Daigueperce (Marcelin's son), Emile Munier, Julien Roiseux and Paul Holderbach, all mentioned by Dr. Gustav Pazaurek in his 1901 publication, *Moderne Gläser*, for their contribution to Gallé's success at the 1900 Exposition Universelle. Several employees, in fact, were awarded individual prizes by the Jury at the Exposition, including Hestaux, Auguste Herbst, and the chemist, Daniel Schoen. The catalogues for the 1903 and 1904 Ecole de Nancy exhibitions in Paris and Nancy list the firm's foremost glass artists at the time as follows:

Director: Emile Lang; Painters: Hestaux, Nicolas, Holderbach; Glass masters: Gillet, Roiseux, Meyer, etc.; Chief decorator: Emile Munier; Engravers: Ismael Soriot, Schmitberger, Mlle Rose Wild, Mercier, *père et fils*, Lang, *père*

For the daily administration of the works, Gallé drew, among others, on Clara Moeller (?-1893), and on his father, Charles Gallé (1818-1902). Many artisans stayed on after Gallé's death, some to the First World War, others to the firm's closure. In 1920 some of the older decorators faithful to the pure Gallé tradition rebelled against the avalanche of industrial wares under production and set up their own small workshop. Under the supervision of Emile Nicholas, blank *vases en double* (two-layered glassware) were commissioned from the nearby St. Louis glasshouse. These were decorated by Windeck and Villermeaux and then etched by Florentin to be marketed under the trade name 'D'Argental'. When bankruptcy forced the enterprise to close, Villermeaux and Florentin returned to their previous employment at the Gallé works.

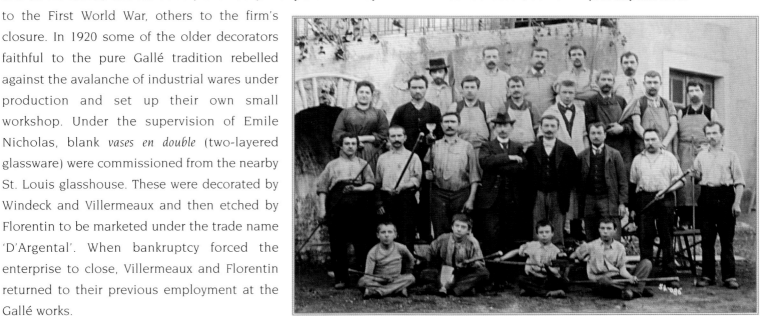

Undated photograph of Gallé with his team of glassblowers, probably late 1890s

L' écaille florale de l'iris, adaption of a vase into a table lamp, 1900 Exposition Universelle

From Art Glass to Lamps

By the late 1890s, electricity's domination of the domestic lighting market was effectively complete; practically all of the design constraints inherent in the use of such traditional combustion fuels as kerosene, oil and paraffin had been eliminated. No longer did a lamp's components dictate its shape. Gone was the need for a vertical flame and a fuel reservoir; the latter, a bulky encumbrance that had somehow to be incorporated into the fixture's overall design. Gas, long a viable alternative source of illumination, was clean, easy to use, and smokeless, but it, too, contained a vertical flame that represented a fire hazard and that had, therefore, to be housed in a glass chimney. This, in turn, prevented the light source from being positioned at an angle, let alone inverted, as it could be with an incandescent filament bulb.

Perhaps word of electricity's advancement came slowly to France's outer provinces, including Alsace-Lorraine, leaving Gallé and his cohorts in the Ecole de Nancy unsure of its practicality and benefits. Nowhere in the surviving documentation of the Gallé firm is there evidence that he had designed combustion or gas light fixtures any earlier; perhaps, he did not initially consider lighting as an artistic extension of his work as a *verrier*. When he did, finally, embrace the medium, towards 1900, he was playing catch-up with fellow members of the annual Paris Salons.

Gallé's apparent uncertainty, and therefore reluctance, on how best to expand his glassware repertoire into the relatively new field of electric lighting – perhaps through his apprehension about how to incorporate the incandescent filament bulb to maximum effect within his designs – is shown in one of the lamps he displayed at the 1900 Exposition Universelle. In this, he took an existing vase – a large organic vessel entitled *l'écaille florale de l'iris* executed in marquéterie-sur-verre with applied and incised detailing and surface patination – and transformed it into a lamp by inserting one bulb within the vessel's interior and another into its bronze stopper (*bouchon*). The critic Pierre-Emile Nicolas described the conversion of the vase into a lamp in his review of the glassware shown at the 1900 Exposition,

> *"Voici une parfaite adaptation de l'écaille florale de l'iris à l'éclairage électrique, au crystal mosaiqué et au bronze. Avant l'anthèse, la fleur des iridacées est continue dans un petit sac fait d'une membrane presque translucide traverse de nervures. C'est cette spathe, comme disent les botanistes, qui a servi de motif à la lampe merveilleuse qui nous occupe. L'anse est formée par une feuille et un bouton floral, très logiquement adaptés, en bronze ciselé ainsi que le socle. Les parois de cette lampe sont en crystal jade mosaiqué de fleurs et de feuilles au milieu desquelles est inscrite cette pensée: Lumière, tu ne seras pas éteinte' … Un dispositif special permet d'allumer à la fois une ampoule électrique dans le bouchon et une autre dans le vase lui-même"…. M. Gallé a crée ainsi plusieurs lampes qui sortent d'une manière bien tranchée des types connus. Comme on le voit, partout ou son génie créateur l'à pousse, partout il s'est éfforcé de ne pas suivre les sentiers battus".*
> ('M. Emile Gallé à l'Exposition de 1900. La verrerie'. *La Lorraine*, 1er Janvier, 1901, p 7).

["This provides a perfect adaption of the floral tortoiseshell iris into electric lighting, in crystal mosaic and bronze. Before anthesis, the flower of the iris continues into a small almost translucent membrane sac lined with ribs. This is the spathe, as it is called by botanists, which serves as the motif of the marvellous lamp in question. The handle is formed from a leaf and a flower bud, very logically adapted in gilded bronze as is the

Opposite: *L'ecaille florale de l'ris* table lamp in marquetry glass, c. 1900. The bronze mount incorporates light sockets within the body of the vessel and in its stopper

Top Left: Sketch of floral light fixtures, published 1903

Top Right: Table lamp in blown glass with wrought-iron mount, published 1903

Bottom: Sketch of light fixtures in blown and etched glass, published 1903

base. The surface of this lamp is a crystal jade mosaic depiciting flowers and leaves, at the centre of which is inscribed this thought: *Light, you will not be extinguished* ... A special mechanism enables light to emit at the same time from an electric bulb within the stopper and another from within the vase itself ... Monsieur Gallé has created so many lamps that come in all manner of distinct styles. As can be seen, in whatever direction his creative genius pushes him, he tries always not to follow the beaten path."]

Pages from a sales catalogue, entitled *Cristallerie et Ebenisterie d'Art d'Emile Gallé a Nancy*, published by the Gallé firm on September 13, 1927, showing a selection of the light fixtures it offered at this late stage of its existence

Clearly, this was a transitional measure, a hesitant if not concessionary first step for Gallé along the road to his eventual full embrace of the lighting medium.

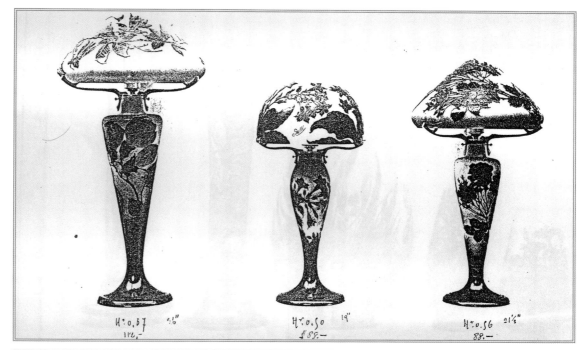

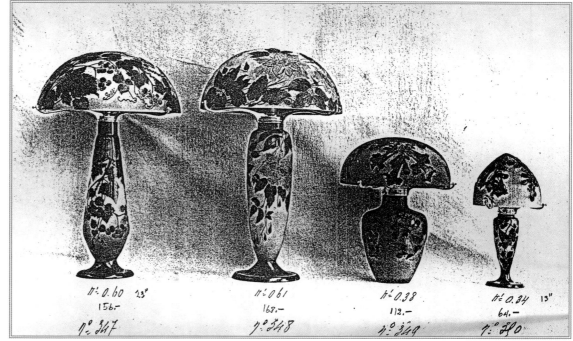

Wall sconce, chandelier and table lamp in moulded glass with etched and enamelled ornamentation. Atypical of the firm's lighting production, these were presumably created at some point in the 1890s when the enamelling technique played a more significant role in Gallé's decorative repertoire of both glass and ceramics than it did at the turn-of-the-century and later

Chapter 2:

LAMPS PRODUCED DURING GALLÉ'S LIFETIME (MID-1890s – 1904)

The following pages include images of lamp models, which, based on surviving period illustrations and literature, are believed to have been created during Gallé's lifetime. After his death in September, 1904, all were systematically phased out and individual or limited edition artworks were replaced with longer runs of standardised industrial glassware. Unique pieces, and those produced *en petit série*, proved to be unprofitable due to the disproportionate amount of time and labour incurred in their production. Then there was the ethical issue of whether such works should continue to be marketed under the name of the *maître verrier* after his death. In anticipation of questions or legal challenges from competitors on this, Gallé's widow, Henriette, determined to add a star to signatures applied to the firm's glassware after 1904 to identify those works produced posthumously, a policy that she implemented in 1905, and which surviving firm records indicate was discontinued only at the advent of WWI. (The star signature is today rarely found on the firm's glassware, however, suggesting either that its application was sporadic and shorter-lived or that later owners had the star removed to increase the work's market value.)

Corolla Lamps

A flower's corolla presented a ready motif: its full-throated symmetrical form serving both as the body for a flowerform vessel and, when set internally with an incandescent filament bulb, a table lamp. This, when lit, emitted a soft internal glow that highlighted the etched tracery of veins within its petals. Several of the bronze bases on Gallé's corolla lamp models warrant note as they are neo-classical in inspiration – some of stepped square form cast with Louis XVI and Restauration motifs – contrary to his standard repertoire of organic themes.

Plate 1.1.

Plate 1.2.

Plate 1.3.

Plate 1.4.

Plate 1.5.

Plate 1.6.

Plate 1.7.

Plate 1.8.

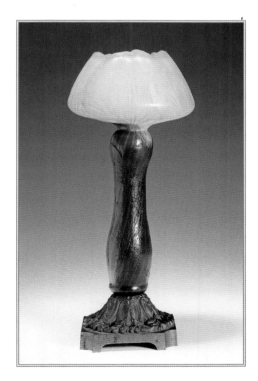

Plate 1.9.

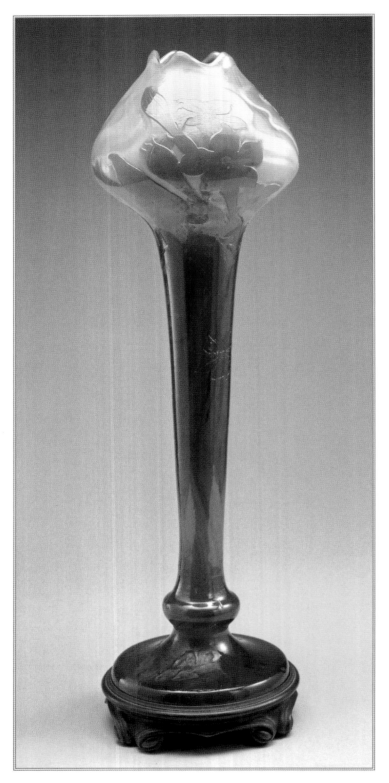

Plate 1.10.

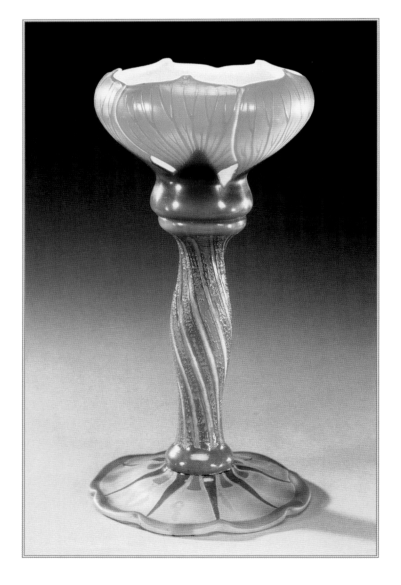

Plate 1.11.

Plate I.12.

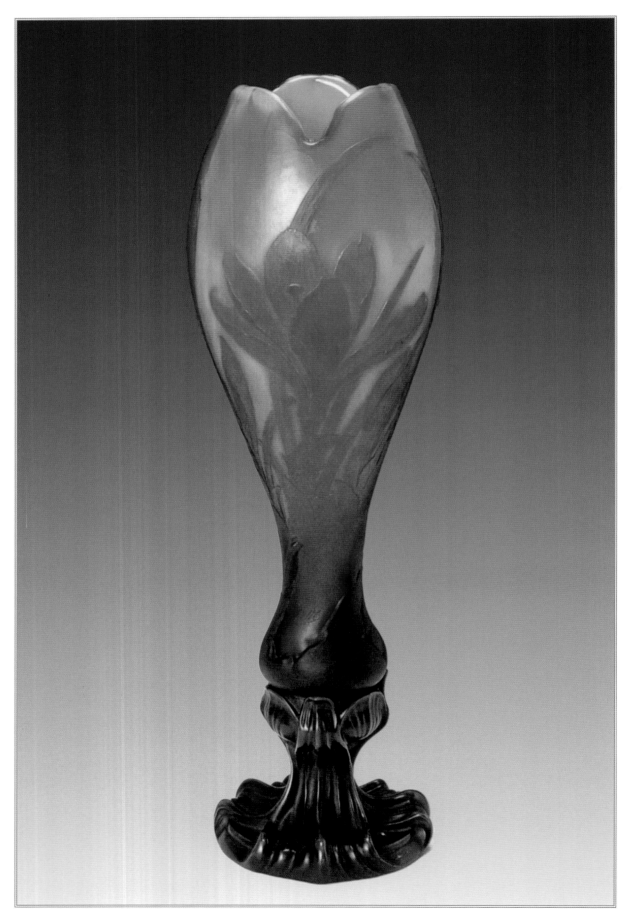

Plate I.13.

Plate 1.14.

Plate 1.15.

Plate 1.16.

Plate 1.17.

Globes

Included here is a selection of the floral globes produced by the Gallé firm to house the single or clustered light bulbs on its various early lamps. Most of these were interchangeable between models. In cased two- or three-layered glass, more complex examples contained *intercalaire* patterning and the engraved veined and textured surface finishes of the species they replicated.

Plate 2.1.

Plate 2.2.

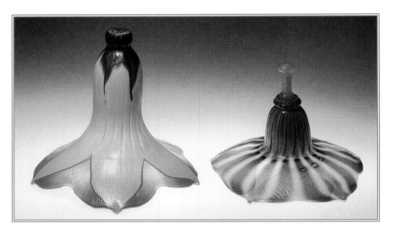

Plate 2.3.

Plate 2.4.

Plate 2.5.

Plate 2.6.

Plate 2.7.

Plate 2.8.

Plate 2.9.

Miscellaneous

The lamp models on the following pages are thought to have been manufactured during Gallé's lifetime, one example having made its public debut at the Exposition of the Ecole de Nancy in Nancy, which opened two months after his death in September, 1904. The majority include bronze or wrought-iron bases that house glass shades, a combination that was gradually phased out as moulded glass bases with etched decoration replaced the original metalware ones. Amongst the most imposing of the firm's early models were the umbel (*ombel*) and fern (*fougère*) table lamps, both with wrought-iron leaves that spiralled up their columnar stems from a base of tangled foliage. Another inspired model was the single mushroom (*coprin*) table lamp, its fluted cap housed on a glass base intricately engraved in bas relief with a cluster of fungi in a dank forest undergrowth realistically enhanced with random splashes of surface patination.

Plate 3.1.

Plate 3.2.

Plate 3.3.

Plate 3.4.

Plate 3.5.

Plate 3.6.

Plate 3.7.

Plate 3.8.

Plate 3.9.

Plate 3.10.

Plate 3.11.

Plate 3.12.

Plate 3.13.

Plate 3.14.

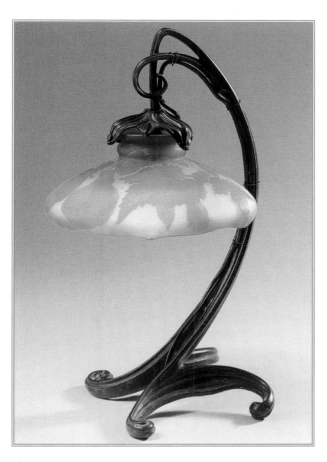

Plate 3.15.

Plate 3.16.

Plate 3.17.

Plate 3.18.

Plate 3.19.

Plate 3.20.

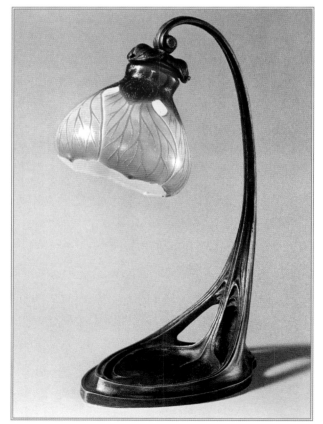

Plate 3.21.

Plate 3.22.

Plate 3.23.

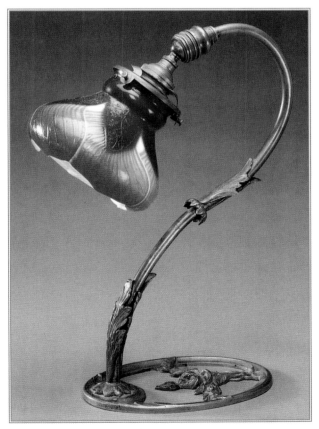

Plate 3.24.

Plate 3.25.

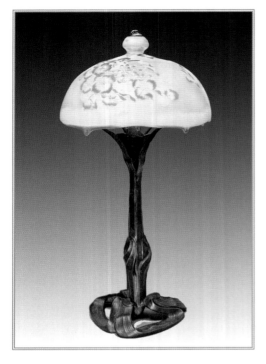

Plate 3.26.

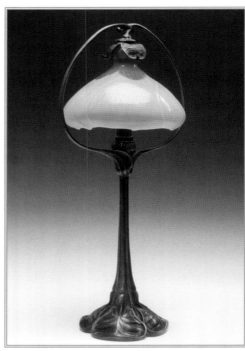

Plate 3.27.

Plate 3.28.

Plate 3.29.

Plate 3.30.

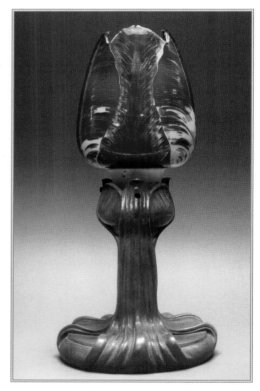

Plate 3.31.

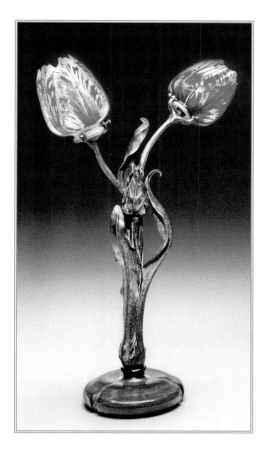

Plate 3.32.

Plate 3.33.

Plate 3.34.

Plate 3.35.

Plate 3.36.

Plate 3.37.

Plate 3.38.

Plate 3.39.

Plate 3.40.

Plate 3.41.

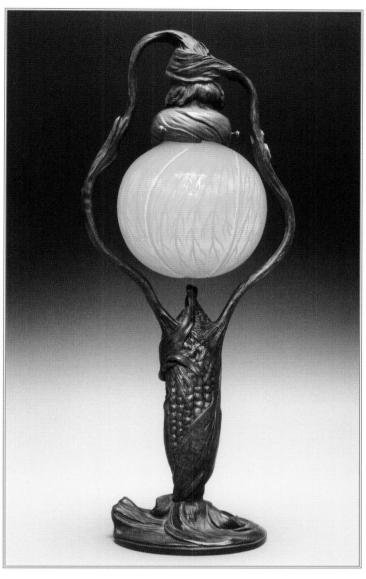

Plate 3.42.

Plate 3.43.

Chapter 3:

THE POST-1904 ERA

This chapter provides insights into a largely undocumented period of the Gallé firm's history, from the death of its founder in 1904 to its closure in 1931, in part by information taken from a speech delivered to the Montreal Glasfax Society in 1974 by René Dezavelle, an employee in the firm's glassworks in the 1920s.

Following Gallé's death in 1904, his widow, Mme Henriette Gallé, placed the direction of the firm under one of her sons-in-law, Dr. Paul Perdrizet, at the time a Professor of Oriental languages at the University of Paris. She explained her decision in a circular to clients: "I have the honour to inform you that, following the sad death of my husband, with whose works I have always been associated, I have made the decision to retain all his employees: designers, modellers, engravers, sculptors and artisans. With the help of these devoted collaborators and thanks to the inexhaustible collection of projects and studies accumulated by Gallé himself, I shall continue to produce the works of art and the techniques that have made him renowned". On Mme Gallé's death in 1914, an article in L'*Etoile de l'Est* explained that she had made this decision in 1904 solely to preserve the livelihoods of the workers, whose numbers had swollen by 1914 to 540, double that of 1901.

In order to keep the firm operational, hard business decisions had to be made by Gallé's successors: initially Dr. Perdrizet, then a triumvirate of all three sons-in-law – Dr. Perdrizet, M.

Gallé's staff in front of the firm's *cristallerie*. Gallé is in the front right foreground. c. 1890

Photograph of the Gallé *cristallerie*, showing the extension on the right begun in the mid-1890s

Workers clearing brush outside the extension building, after 1900

Chevalier, a spun silk manufacturer in the Vosges mountains, and Professor Lucien Bourgogne, a professor of Literature at the Sorbonne. The factory closed at the beginning of the First World War, reopening after the armistice, at which point the decision was made to concentrate production on editions of smaller glassware; large-sized items had proven to be too costly and did not sell readily. The decision to manufacture assembly-line items only was no doubt sound; without the guiding genius and inspiration of its creator, no other course was commercially viable for the firm.

Gallé had begun experimenting with acid-etching in the mid-1880s to supplement the time-consuming technique of wheel-engraving. He explained his truce with industrial production, hugely reluctant but pragmatic, in his Notes to the Jury at the 1889 Exposition Universelle:

"Applications industrielles, Vulgarisation artistique. – En vous soumettant, Messieurs, après des œuvres raffinées et luxueuses, les spécimens de ma fabrication adaptée à des besoins plus modestes, il ne me semble pas déchoir. Ni moi, ni mes ouvriers, nous n'avons trouvé impossible la conciliation de la production a bon marché et de l'art; nous n'avons pas pensé que la robe commerciale du crystal dut être nécessairement de mauvais gout. … Je ne me suis pas soucié seulement de faire œuvre de maitrise, j'ai voulu encore rendre l'art accessible, de façon à préparer un nombre mois restreint d'esprits à gouter les œuvres plus enveloppées. J'ai propagé la setiment de la nature, celui de la grâce des fleurs, de la beauté des insectes. Mon labeur de vingt-quatre années déjà a mis au jour dans la fabrication fantaisiste verrerie un nombre considérable de formes, des modèles, d'idées, de genres infiniment varies. Je puis me présenter devant vous comme un vulgarisateur de l'art. Vous trouvez chez moi les preuves que l'art ni le gout ne sont dans la dépendance de façons couteuses, et qu'il suffit au producteur de soumettre avec grace et sentiment personnel ses modèles et ses décors a la destination économique et au travail pratique du métier. Dans ma production a bon marche, j'ai évité le faux, le biscornu, le fragile. J'ai employé des colorations solides. Des creations incessantes ont influence le gout du public moyen. J'ai ouvert a la cristallerie et prépare, quelquefois a mon détriment, des voies fructueuses a des usines pour la très grande production …" (Ecrits pour l'art, 1980 reprint, p. 349).

["Industrial applications, artistic popularisation – in submitting, Gentlemen, works in the style of refined and luxury items, my works do not neglect to cater to more modest needs. Neither I nor my workers found it impossible to reconcile cheap production and art; we saw no reason that commercial crystal pieces need be of bad taste... I did not care to create only master works, I wanted to make art more accessible, sometimes spending a number of months attempting to distil the essence of the most sophisticated works. I explored the theme of nature; the grace of flowers, the beauty of insects. My work of twenty-four years already updated in the manufacture of fancy glassware in a considerable number of forms, patterns, ideas and genres, all infinitely varied. So I can stand before you as a populariser of the art. You will find in my atelier the evidence that art is neither a matter of taste, that it is dependent on costly production methods, and that is enough for the manufacturer to submit his models and settings with grace and sensitivity to their economic destination and to practical work practices. In my low-cost production I avoided the fake, the quirky, the fragile. I have used plain colours. The continuing creations have influenced public taste. I opened the glassworks and prepared, sometimes to my own detriment, possible manufacturing processes to enable large-scale production ..."]

Marquetry panel designed by Auguste Herbst depicting the front of the Gallé cristallerie. Collection Musée d'Ecole de Nancy

Illustration in *Deutsche Kunst und Dekoration*, 1904, of a cameo glass lamp with extended electrical cord

Further illustration of an early cameo lamp, c. 1902

Cameo glass lamp, illustrated in *Deutsche Kunst und Dekoration*, 1904

In short, etching was not a technique that would enhance Gallé's artistic reputation. One of his exhibits at the 1889 Exposition, a small four-layered vase decorated with pink roses on a black, brown and white ground, was described in the firm's catalogue solely as 'cameo'. It was probably an early example of wheel-engraving used in conjunction with etching, the latter's presence carefully disguised by the engraver in his finishing operation.

Gallé, the consummate artist, was forced to transform himself into a pragmatic businessman. Only by mass-producing an inexpensive range of commercial glassware could he generate the capital necessary to keep the firm profitable. The key to this was acid-etching. In 1906, Roger Marx drew attention to the fact that the very same problem had forced Gallé to industrialise his cabinetry workshops in 1894 when he wrote in *La Revue universelle: litterature et beaux-arts* of the two-tier quality of Gallé's furniture: "Whereas a select number of pieces were designed for museums, others were vulgar, commercial and industrial, assembled with measured economy to reach every home." The sad reality was that the revenue generated by Gallé's commercial glassware and furniture was indispensable to the firm's operation, in large part subsidizing the disproportionate amount of time and the artisanship spent on experimentation and *pièces uniques* in both media. So, despite Gallé's aversion to a process that lacked the precision and artistic dexterity required of the manual operation, acid-etching had been in full commercial use by the mid-1890s. Numerous etched pieces were illustrated in monthly art revues at the time, particularly *Deutsche Kunst und Dekoration* and the *Magazine of Art*, the former presenting a selection of cameo table lamps that showed Gallé, like many of his contemporaries, had no ready solutions at first to the unsightly tangle of light sockets and cords that carried power to the newly commercialized *Fee électricité*.

The Acid-Etching Technique

Gallé's etching process was described in the scientific journal *La Nature* in 1913. Fundamentally unchanged from its introduction roughly 28 years earlier, it remained in operation until the firm's closure in 1931. Today, such pieces are generally referred to in the marketplace as 'industrial Gallé'.

Once the choice of colours for a series of glassware had been determined, batches of each were placed in separate crucibles in a Boetius coke-burning furnace and heated to melting point (1400-1450°C / 2552-2642°F). The first colour was then gathered on a pipe and blown on to the marver where it was rolled flat. The second colour was similarly gathered and rolled on top of the first. Each additional colour – seldom more than four – was superimposed in this manner.

The layered mass of glass was then re-heated and blown into a wooden mould. This, fashioned in the cabinet-makers shop, was made of two hinged sections that were opened when the shaped piece (all mould-blown items, such as bowls, lamp shades and bases, were similarly manufactured) had been slowly annealed in the lehr (a temperature-controlled kiln).

The piece of glass was next transferred to a draughtsman-decorator who traced the chosen motif – usually floral or a continuous landscape – on to it with an indelible white pencil, carefully indicating which parts were to be removed by etching, and which not.

For large editions, especially after 1918, the procedure was standardised. The design, sketched beforehand by a master designer, was transferred on to a transparent wax pattern paper, which was then pierced with tiny dots. The pattern paper template was then wrapped around the piece and a white powder sprinkled on to it and rubbed into the holes. When the paper was removed, the outline of the design was visible on the glass surface, providing the decorator with a key by which to apply his acid-resistant paint. The application of the powder, paint and acid, followed

Glass artisans applying Judean bitumen to mask those areas of the design on the glass vessel that were not to be etched when it was next immersed in an acid bath. Illustrated in *La Nature*, 1913

View of the decorating studio, showing a row of glass artisans at their work benches; behind them editions of acid-etched glassware

by polishing as a final step, took roughly one-and-a-half days for each piece of glass. (In his early experiments with the process, Gallé had had three similar designs made up, from which he would, after lengthy examination, retain one and destroy the others.)

The piece was now ready for one of the *verriers*, who were seated on stools in long rows lining the brightly lit *atelier*. Heavy pieces were assigned to the men and lighter ones to the women. Each *verrier* was equipped with a mug of Judean bitumen (a resinous acid-resistant paste), brushes and rags. The vase was positioned on a wooden bar and secured with one hand while the liquid bitumen was applied with a brush to mask out the parts to be retained. It was then immersed in a large lead-lined bath of hydrofluoric acid. The progress of the acid as it ate its way into the surface of the glass was carefully monitored, its *agressivité* ("biting power") determined in the laboratory beforehand to match the hardness of the glass. Next, the piece was removed from the bath and washed and dried before being returned to the *verrier* for a further application of bitumen.

This process was repeated until each successive layer had been thinned down, penetrated in spots or totally removed. Finally, the piece was transferred to a polisher to be buffed on an emery wheel. This removed defects such as ragged edges, mould seams and remaining traces of acid. Today, this technique is commonly referred to as "wheel polishing" or "fire polishing". Certain pieces, for special effect, would be given a final diluted acid bath to give the etched ground a matt finish, thus increasing the contrast between the primary and secondary areas of design.

Gallé industrial glassware varies widely in quality. Early pieces, especially, were superbly rendered, to the extent that they are often almost indistinguishable from wheel-carved examples in their sharpness of detail and subtle colour gradations.

Gallé's initial dislike of the etching process gave way to guarded approval as his *verriers* mastered the nuances of the acid bath. Special effects were introduced: the veining of leaves and pitting of tree trunks soon seemed more realistic than nature, as did the light *grisaille* patterning that could be applied to backgrounds. A charming variation were random flower sprays etched on the interior of a vessel or lampshade, surprising and delighting the viewer when internally illuminated.

The process's main function was, however, to produce a huge volume of industrial wares, such as lamps, chandeliers, brush-holders and vases, at competitive prices. Shapes were continually modified to provide variety: many lampshades were domed, others crown-shaped or conical. Bases were mostly of baluster form, others sharply-shouldered or globular. The majority, however, were by definition of average quality, hurried through the factory to retail outlets in Frankfurt, Paris and London.

Towards 1910, quality was downgraded as costs were pared. The lavish four- and three-layered cameo vases of yesteryear were systematically eliminated; retained were a series of two-layered models depicting flora and landscapes. Large vases were manufactured in editions of ten dozen; *bonbonnières*, trays and small bibelots in twenty- to thirty-dozen editions. Editions of lamps, often

After the acid-etching process was completed, any surviving defects, such as rough edges and mould seams, on the vessel's surface were polished off on an emery wheel

Plates 4.1 and Plate 4.2. These two lamps, at 31½in./80cm. represent the largest table lamps manufactured by the Gallé glassworks

produced in two or three sizes, were smaller still. Shortly before the First World War a series of vases and lamps were decorated with panoramas of the Vosges mountain chain and the Gerardment, Longemer and Retournemer lakes. These were engraved with a defiant, jingoistic slogan that would soon return to haunt Germany: 'This vessel, decorated with the gold and blue of the Vosges mountains, from where arise the lamentations of the vanquished, symbolises the loss of Alsace-Lorraine in 1870'. Not surprisingly, when the models were reissued in 1918, the inscription was deemed redundant and therefore removed. Two-colour permutations for etched glassware became the norm in the post-war years: landscapes with perennials, lakes and mountains were issued in bluish tones; those with bushes, trees and meadows in green ones. Later still, a muted, autumnal palette was introduced: grey, forest green, brown, amber and burgundy.

Plate 4.3. A panorama of the mountainscape in rural Alsace-Lorraine

Plate 4.4. Peony table lamp

Plate 4.5. Hydrangea table lamp, from the same mould as the Peony lamp seen opposite

Plate 4.6. Magnolia

Plate 4.7. Magnolia

Plate 4.8. Hibiscus

Plate 4.9.

The dates of manufacture of the largest Gallé cameo lamps – such as the wisteria, chrysanthemum, peony, lemon tree, magnolia, hydrangea and laburnum models – remain unrecorded. Of formidable size with large domed shades on baluster bases with matching floral ornamentation, many of these three- or four-layered designs are strikingly beautiful, rendered in a blended naturalistic palette often with dabs of additional colour applied on the interior of the shade to highlight flower centres or buds.

Plate 4.10. Lemon tree table lamp

Plate 4.11.

Plate 4.12. Wisteria table lamp

Mould-Blown Glassware

The term 'mould-blown' or *soufflé* is generally used today to distinguish between Gallé industrial glassware that has relief detailing and that which does not. Whereas in both instances the shape of the vessel was formed in a mould, in a mould-blown piece the primary decoration protrudes significantly from the surface to provide sculpted definition and, thereby, increased realism (see pp.62-63).

The technique was limited almost exclusively to a series of cameo vases and light fixtures decorated with vegetables and fruit, to which it was well suited. Apples and pendent bunches of cherries stand out naturalistically against pale matte skies, each domed piece of fruit highly polished and with internal luminosity. Others in the series included plums, crocuses, tulips, tomatoes, hyacinths, fuchsias, water lilies, morning glories and rambler roses. Fruit-laden orange and lemon branches embellish the underside of a pair of chandeliers, on which a squirrel forages for acorns on an oak bough. The most prized mould-blown model today, however, is the rhododendron table lamp, produced with either red or purple blossoms, every bit as stunning with the additional interplay of blended colours generated by their relief detailing. The model is believed to have been exhibited at the 1925 Exposition Universelle, Paris. Smaller lamp models in this genre included the mould-blown cherry and plum designs (see overleaf).

Most mould-blown pieces comprised three or more superimposed layers of coloured glass, each compounding the luminescent effect. The etching technique, employing hydrofluoric acid, was the same as that used for standard industrial wares, superimposed colours within editions being interchanged to widen the range of effects.

Plate 5.1.

Plate 5.2.

Plate 5.3. Rhododendron table lamp in a rare variant colour, the same model as Plates 5.4 and 5.5

Plate 5.4. Rhododendron

Plate 5.5. Rhododendron

Plate 5.6. Mould-blown cherry table lamp

It was assumed when the Art Nouveau revival began in the 1970s that the mould-blown process was introduced during Gallé's lifetime, or soon thereafter. However, *Ecrits pour l'Art*, the collection of his writings published posthumously in 1908, makes no mention of this kind of relief decoration, which would have been a most uncharacteristic omission for the fastidious Gallé, whose concern with precedence drove him to tabulate all his inventions. The mystery was solved in M. Dezavelle's 1974 speech: the entire mould-blown series was introduced in the years 1924-1925, in anticipation of the 1925 Exposition Universelle, where a wide selection was displayed. Included in the designs presented to promote the technique was that most uncharacteristic of Gallé wares, the 'elephant' vase.

Although the 1925 Exposition sparked a fresh batch of lamp and vase models by the Gallé firm,

Plate 5.7. Mould-blown cherry table lamp

these appeared at the time dreadfully tired and outmoded. It is hard even to comprehend now why they were displayed in an exhibition dedicated to post-war design. The firm's booth was rightly passed over by the critics, ecstatic about the technical virtuosities of Maurice Marinot and André Thuret. Lalique's commercial glassware, similarly in the modernist idiom, likewise captured the period's mood with its achromatic palette. A sales catalogue published in September, 1927, appears to have served as the *cristallerie*'s last marketing promotion. It closed in 1931, the factory converted into a technical school for electricians The Magasin de la rue de la Faiencerie in Nancy, which had always carried Gallé's wares, continued to do so until 1935. In the same year, Eugène Corbin made the donation that established the Lorraine Museum of Modern Decorative Arts, today Le Musée de l'Ecole de Nancy.

Chapter 4:

DESIGN ELEMENTS

Lamp Mounts

Gallé used mounts sparingly on his early glassware, preferring that the piece be freestanding or rest on an applied glass or wood foot, the latter often carved with foliate decoration to provide a decorative fillip. Later mounts in bronze or wrought iron, which replaced wood due to their durability and visual lightness, show that in time he came to view these as an integral part of the total composition. In one example, trailing bronze seaweed spirals upwards to encircle a marine vase, terminating in crested waves that encase its freeform mount. In another, a slender leaf emerges from a bed of tangled foliage to trace the contours of the cylindrical glass stem of a table lamp base, providing both structural support and an increased naturalistic effect.

With few exceptions, the mounts on the firm's light fixtures were produced in the same small metal workshop and foundry in which the firm's furniture mounts were cast. Bronze dragonflies and bats, frozen in flight, were assigned either to support glass incense burners and *veilleuses* or to adorn the pull handles and key escutcheons on the frieze drawers of the firm's marquetry desks. Messrs. Heck and Roth were listed in 1904 as the firm's metal mount specialists.

Several important glass commissions incorporated intricate bronze mounts, some which were themselves adorned with encrusted glass jewels: in the 1890s, the Cattleya vase offered to the Empress of Russia and a cornet inspired by a Victor Hugo verse, L'*Etoile du matin, l'étoile du soir*. In 1903, several Salon pieces were similarly enhanced: *le chêne, le lierre, urne agate*, and *gourde aux éphémères*. Wrought iron was generally preferred to bronze for oversized objects, such as two monumental amphora urns – one, commissioned for the wedding of M. Eugène Corbin, is now in the Musée de l'Ecole de Nancy; the other, inspired by King Solomon, was sold at auction in Paris in 1981.

A royal, state or private commission sometimes justified a mount made of precious metal. For these, Gallé turned to the foremost gold- and silversmiths of the day. None appears to have been especially favoured over another; the skills of Cardeilhac, Lucien Falize, Froment-Meurice, Gérard Sandoz, Bonvallet, Jules Cayette and l'Escalier de Cristal were all called upon. The last-mentioned was managed at the turn-of-the-century by the Pannier brothers, who provided numerous mounts for the Gallé glassware offered through their retail shop at 1 rue Aubert, Paris. In the mid-1890s, Gallé retained Fabergé to produce the silver floral mount for a vase presented to the Russian Grand-Duke Serge. A 1902 article by Maurice Demaison in Art *et Décoration* illustrates several fine examples of such Gallé mounts, those in precious metals usually bearing the inscribed name or impressed *poinçon* of the gold- or silversmith.

Left: Period illustration of a table lamp with blown glass shade on a wrought-iron base, 1904

Opposite Page: A model similar in style to that shown in the illustration (left) with a blown glass shade depicting a flowerhead and the wrought-iron base of the stem and leaves

The bases on Gallé's early lamps were modelled mostly in wrought iron or bronze as flower or plant stems rising from a cushion of radiating curled or flattened leaves, their glass shades etched with flora and housed on slender tendrils issuing from the upper section of the stems. These are today seen as pure Art Nouveau confections, designed to create a perfect union of a plant's various components: stem, stalks and blossoms.

A caveat is in order here on the fact that no printed records, including illustrations, have survived to guide today's researcher on the majority of the metal bases produced by the Gallé firm in its early years of lamp production (c. 1897-1905). Absent is any archival documentation on the different base models the firm created, unlike other industrial art manufacturers at the turn-of-the-century, most notably Tiffany Studios, which published lists that identified its bases (and shades) by name and model number. Tiffany lamp bases are impressed in most part on the underside with a 3-digit model number that corresponds to their chronological listing in the firm's publications, providing ready identification in today's marketplace. As a vast number of the metal bases produced by the Gallé factory do not bear impressed signatures or markings, however, this can cause today's collectors to question whether the shades and bases on some Gallé models are correctly matched;

i.e., that they originated together, or that they could constitute the marriage of a base by a contemporary lamp manufacturer on to which a Gallé glass lampshade has later been added (many sculptors and metalworkers at the *fin-de-siècle* designed bases in a similar Art Nouveau organic style to those by Gallé, some displayed at the annual Paris Salons). The problem is further compounded by the fact that it is not today known whether the firm's early bases were designed to be interchangeable with a range of its lampshades or designed to house a single model of shade only. If, for example, the customer chose to place a shade with a specific floral design on a base decorated with a forest scene, or vice versa, would such a switch be implemented? One assumes so, as this would represent a smart marketing strategy, but there is no period proof that the Gallé firm offered this service. Such non-matching combinations appear with some frequency on today's market, leaving open the question of whether the shade or base in the original pairing was at some point broken and subsequently replaced with one of similar form but differently ornamented, as the means to 'complete' the unit.

Above: Mounted perfume burner (*brûle parfum*) and a table lamp, exhibited at the Salon of La Société Nationale des Beaux-Arts, Paris, 1905

Opposite Page: The perfume burner as seen above (with replaced metal mount)

Detail of the Parakeet shade on the Gingko floor base, c.1900

Detail of *Ombellifères* floor lamp shown opposite

Floor Mounts

Evident in these pages is the diverse range of light fixtures that Gallé's firm produced, including table, bedside, hanging and wall models. Curiously, amongst the avalanche of commercial examples marketed through more than three decades, very few floor models were produced, for reasons that are today unclear. Only two, in fact, are now known, both *pièces uniques* on a monumental scale with etched glass shades and moulded glass columnar bases, one mounted in bronze, the other in wrought-iron. One of these, which remained in the Gallé family for many years,

contains a shade around a meter in diameter decorated with numerous yellow and green parakeets perched on the branches of a Gingko-Biloba (maidenhair) tree against an orange sky. The elaborate organic metal decoration on the lamp's base matches that of the Gingko foliage and branches on the shade to provide an impressive unified naturalistic composition (for additional images of the lamp, then in the collection of the American art dealer, Robert Walker, see Philippe Garner, *Emile Gallé*, Rizzoli, 1976, p. 90). The second known example of a floor lamp provides a similar integrated composition based on the separate elements – blossoms, seed pods, stems and leafage – of the umbel plant.

Floor lamp *Ombellifères* with glass shade and column, and wrought-iron mount, c.1900

Motifs

As a young student at the Lycée Impériale in Nancy, Gallé was taught by the well-known and respected botanist Professor Emile Godron, author of *La Flore française* and *La Flore Lorraine*. He continued his botanical studies during his year in Weimar and never lost his deep interest in the forms of Nature. Gallé applied a wide range of botanical motifs to his lamps, just as he did to his art glass and furniture: wild cherries, convolvuli, vines, poppies and orchids grew abundantly, while insects, bats and birds supplied the fauna to the flora.

Umbel

A favourite Gallé lamp motif, common to all of the disciplines in which he worked, was the cow parsley, an umbel (*ombel*) indigenous to Lorraine. The firm's surviving correspondence shows that umbel lamps frequently incorporated the flower on the base *only*; the shade was decorated with butterflies or birds to provide variety. It seems that feedback from the firm's salesmen had determined that potential customers found an overall floral design visually overwhelming.

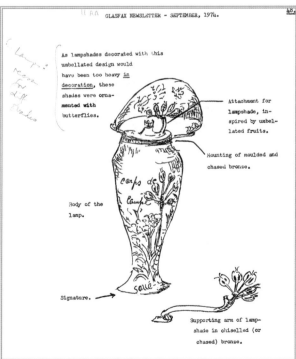

Left: *Ombelle* (*berce des près*) chandelier commissioned for the dining-room in Edouard Hannon's residence, Brussels, c. 1904, comprising 13 shades in blown and etched cameo glass on a bronze mount. Collection Musée des Arts Décoratifs, Paris

Centre: Sketch by René Dezavelle of a Gallé umbel table lamp shown at his slide presentation for the Glasfax Society in Montreal, September, 1974

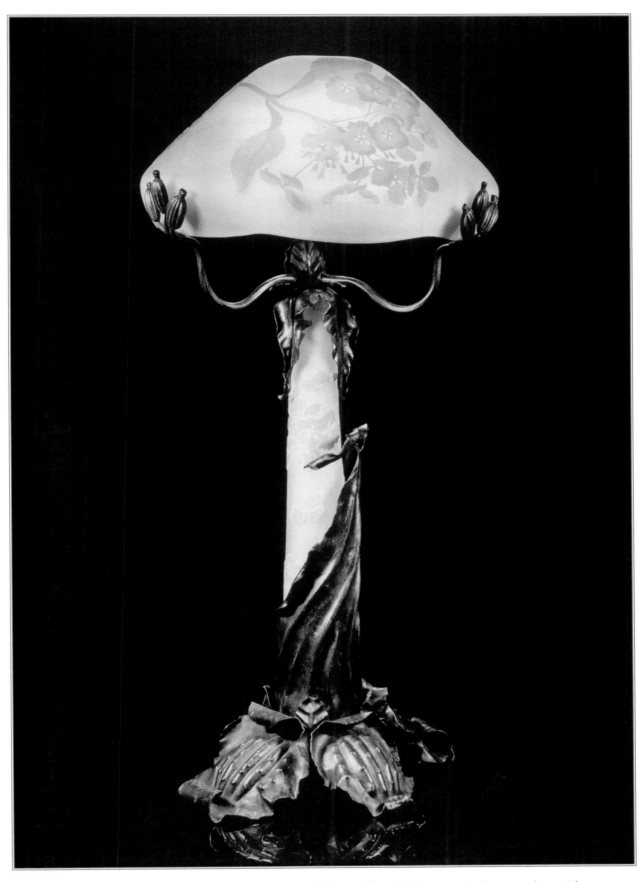

Above and Opposite Page: Variant models of the *Ombelle* table lamp; etched cameo glass with wrought-iron base, the models introduced c. 1903

One of various bat lampshade models produced by the Gallé firm, some of which have additional decoration etched on the interior surface of the shade

Bats

According to René Dezavelle, a former employee of the Gallé glassworks, the model of the bat lamp, today a highly-prized Gallé item, was originally designed with a swarm of black butterflies, their wings haloed with gold and silver, above a line of silhouetted black trees along the shade's lower rim. Very few models sold, as potential clients rejected them on the grounds that the black butterflies symbolized to them neurasthenia, a disorder generating insomnia and headaches! The butterflies were, therefore, replaced by the flight of a beautiful bat so that the tree-line would represent dusk against the orange-red background sky. This effect, in turn, was found to be too dismal and the idea was quickly dropped. Hence the rarity today of this much-prized work of art!

Gourds

In an Art Nouveau context, Gallé's creations reached their apogee between 1900 and 1904, a brief period during which he adapted the shape of much of his glassware to its theme. Vases decorated with lilies became lily-shaped in a marriage of form and function. Fully-ripened gourds pendent on their vines glowed from within at the touch of a switch. Mushroom lamps brought the concept to full embodiment in the metamorphosis of the giant fungi into light fixtures.

Colocynths (*Coloquintes*) wall fixture (*girandole*) in wrought-iron and blown layered glass, c. 1900. Collection Musée de l'Ecole de Nancy

Sketch of a wall fixture similar to that shown, above, perhaps the maquette for it. Collection Musée d'Orsay

Les *Coprins* lamp on an *aux ombelles* pedestal table, exhibited at the *Ecole de Nancy: Exposition d'Art Decoratif*, Nancy, 1903

Coprins

A consummate work in glass, and to many Gallé connoisseurs his ultimate *chef d'oeuvre*, the *Coprins* or mushroom table lamp was created around 1902, reputedly in a small edition to illuminate a patron's dining room furnished like a forest. The lamp's design of clustered Coprini is open to various interpretations, including that it is an allegory for the three ages of man: the smallest fungus, with short stem and closed cap, represents his emerging youth; the middle fungus, with ripened cap, his physical (and sexual) prime; and the largest one, with umbrella-formed cap with decaying rim, his decline into old age. About 32 inches high, the lamp is a technical *tour de force*. The three stems, of which the largest in three known examples is a greenish-gray, perhaps to denote maturity in contrast to the younger blue-tinted ones, were blown in vertically ribbed moulds and applied internally with random flecks of metallic foil. The three caps are in cased glass applied externally with oval wheel cuts that evoke in the viewer the sense of droplets of early morning dew. Select engraved detailing and patination on the surface of the glass add to the realistic effect, which is completed by the leaf-form mount that sprouts from the wrought-iron base. The catalogue accompanying the *Exposition de l'Ecole de Nancy à Strasbourg*, 1908, credited the *Coprins* lamp's design and production to three of Gallé's senior staff: Louis Hestaux, Paul Nicolas, and Paul Holderbach. At least five examples of the model are known, including those at the Musée de l'Ecole de Nancy, the Kitazawa Museum of Art in Japan, and private collections in Germany, Japan, and Korea.

Design by Gallé of leafy branches, probably for a piece of enamelled glassware or a veneered furniture panel, including background clumps of mushrooms (*coprins*), late 1890s

Four examples of *Les Coprins* (Coprini) table lamp, c. 1902-04.

Above: *EMILE GALLÉ Dreams into Glass* exhibition, Corning Museum of Glass, 1984

Right: Christies, Geneva, 11-11-1984

Overleaf left: Collection Kitazawa Museum of Art, Japan

Overleaf right: Sothebys, New York, December 1/2-12-1989

Flora and Fauna

Even a cursory glance through the following pages reveals the infinite thematic shade-and-base combinations introduced by the firm to provide kaleidoscopic snapshots of the outdoors: butterflies, moths, dragonflies, swallows and eagles hover, flutter, glide or swoop over flora and mountain vistas in a seemingly endless interplay of Nature's decorative motifs.

Chapter 5:

WORLD EXPOSITIONS and the ANNUAL PARIS SALONS

Exposition Universelle, Paris, 1900

Though lamps did not feature prominently in Gallé's exhibits at either the Salons or international expositions, one exception was a drawing-room model, entitled *La Solanée*, displayed in 1900; its lace-like conical shade – designed as clematis corymbs – that took its inspiration from a verse by Victor Hugo, *La lumière montera dans tout comme une sève*. Gallé's 1900 exhibition catalogue listed further examples: a wrought-iron chandelier described as *en graines*; a night light entitled *Fleur de Veilleuse*; and a *Fleur de Courge* desk light. Gallé's exhibition catalogue did, however, include a sketch, entitled *Le Jardin de la Lampe* (*Conte arabe*), which provides a tantalizing view of the display in which Gallé planned to show his light fixtures, including two glass vitrines, *Fruit du Mal* and *Fruits de l'Esprit*, inspired by the verse by Saint Matthew, "You will recognise them by their fruits". Curiously, neither the fixtures nor the vitrines were illustrated either in the firm's own literature or in revues by the critics of works at the Exposition, indicating that the display was not included in the Gallé exhibit.

La Solanée table lamp, exhibited at the 1900 Exposition Universelle, Paris

Sketch of the *Le Jardin de la Lampe* display in Gallé's exhibition catalogue for the 1900 Exposition Universelle

The glass furnace, *Les Sept Cruches de Marjolaine*, which Galle installed at the 1900 Exposition Universelle, both to show the public how his glassware was created and to solicit commissions. Of it, the critic Robert de La Sizeranne wrote, *Enfin attendez un peu de temps encore aupres de la vitrine du maitre-verrier, et lorsque la nuit sera venue, regardez s'allumer autour du four les sept ballons de verre qu'il a intitules les Sept cruches de Marjolaine. ... Mais quand nous aurons contemple les sept verres ou apparaissent les sept couleurs de l'arc-en-ciel, nous penserons que M. Galle a fait mieux que le magician de la legend* ("L'Art a l'Exposition de 1900, Avons-nous un style moderne?", *Revue des Deux-Mondes*, 15 Octobre, 1900)

[Finally, let us linger a little while near the showcase of the glass master and when the dusk is setting in, look around the oven and see the seven balloons of glass named "The Seven Jugs of Marjolaine" by the artist.
But, when we contemplate the seven vessels on which we see the seven colours of the rainbow appear, we must agree that Mr. Gallé has managed better then the magician of the legend.]

Exposition de l'Ecole de Nancy, Paris, 1903

The Ecole de Nancy became a legal entity on 13 February, 1901, with Gallé as president and Louis Majorelle, Eugene Vallin and Antonin Daum as vice-presidents, its primary mission the renaissance, development and promotion of the industrial arts in the provinces of Alsace-Lorraine. Whereas its members had enjoyed a loose inter-disciplinary affiliation since 1894, their broad individual success at the 1900 Exposition Universelle in Paris invited a formal association. The first test of this newly-forged union came at the 1903 Paris Salon, staged at the Pavillon de Marsan, where the group exhibited together across a wide range of the decorative arts. The accompanying exhibition catalogue showed in the members' artworks the stylistic bond they held with nature, that which had spawned the Art Nouveau movement a decade earlier. Gallé's exhibit included furniture, glassware and lamps, the last-mentioned including an umbel (*ombel*) table model, its cameo glass shade and column supported by a spiralling leafy wrought-iron mount raised on a tangled bed of foliage.

Gallé's love and knowledge of botany requires more than a passing nod. Early tuition under Professor D.A. Godron, author of *La Flore française* and *La Flore lorraine* sparked in him an encyclopedic knowledge of flowers, one evident in his sketches of orchids, published in *La Lorraine* in 1904, from which he transferred the flowers into working drawings and from there onto glass. A close working relationship with the Nancy botanist and geneticist, Victor Lemoine, who was especially renowned for a new species of primula, and with Charles Schultze, Gallé's own gardener at La Garenne, the family home, filled his spare time.

Roger Marx, Inspector General of French Museums and an irrepressible Gallé publicist since his earliest days, stressed the Nanceien's bond with Nature in an obituary in *Le Bulletin des Sociétés Artistiques de l'Est*, 'He was an exquisitely sensitive poet, who lived in the midst of nature in a state of perpetual excitement, drawing decorative ideas from this great mistress of all artists and developing them through his own fertile imagination. The flora and fauna of his own region were the source of thousands of delicate and ingenious images, on which he elaborated with wonderful spirit'.

Period illustration of a table lamp exhibited at the Exposition de l'Ecole de Nancy, Paris, 1903

Opposite left: *Aux Ombelles* electric lamp for the Umbel bedroom

Opposite centre: Selection of light fixtures exhibited at the Exposition de l'Ecole de Nancy, Paris, 1903

Opposite right: Bedroom *Ombellifères* (La Berce des Près), in collaboration with Auguste Herbst and Paul Holderbach. Illustrated in L'Art Décoratif, Janvier, 1903, p.177. Note the two lamps to the right of the image

Recent illustration of the table lamp exhibited at the Exposition de l'Ecole de Nancy, Paris, 1903

Salon of La Société Nationale des Beaux Arts, 1904

A year later, in the Ecole de Nancy exhibition at the same venue, two further important examples were introduced: *Les Coprins* and *Fleurs de palmier austral*, the latter an uncharacteristic depiction of a palm bough, its shade composed of strands of bead-like blossoms falling from a curved bronze branch.

Unfortunately, many of these early lamp models, produced either as unique creations or *en petite serie*, included such loosely-secured and fragile components as crystal beads or blown glass shades with thin wavy lower rims. These simply begged at some point when moved or cleaned to incur damage and, therefore, had little chance of surviving through the years in pristine condition. Whereas some have emerged on occasion into the marketplace with replaced components or in modified form, most now exist only in period illustrations.

Left: *Les Coprins* lamp on *Les Ombellules* guéridon. Illustrated in *L'Art Décoratif*, Janvier-Juin, 1905, p.97

Below left: Glassware exhibited at the *Ecole de Nancy: Exposition d' Art Décoratif*, hosted by La Société Lorraine des Amis des Arts, Nancy, 1904, including, front row, second from left, the *Fleurs de palmier austral* lamp with pendent beaded crystal shades

Below right: The *Fleurs de palmier austral* lamp, which was included in the Ecole de Nancy exhibition of 1904, shown on the *Nocturne* commode, illustrated in *L'Art Décoratif*, 1904, p. 103

Opposite: Variant model of the lamp shown on the right of the *Fleurs de palmier austral* lamp in the period illustration (below left)

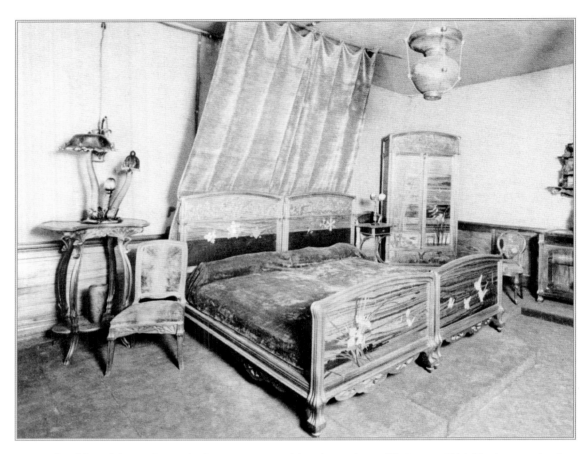

Views of Gallé's exhibit at the Ecole de Nancy's Exposition d'Art Décoratif in Nancy, 1904-05, show a selection of his lamps interspersed with major pieces of his furniture, including the *Aube et Crepescule* bed and the *Vitrine aux Libellule* commissioned by a major client, Henry Hirsch

Ecole de Nancy: Exposition d'Art Décoratif, Nancy, 1904-05

The catalogue for the L'Ecole de Nancy's exposition in Nancy in 1904, which opened after Gallé's death in September that year, listed more illuminated works in his glassware entry than in any other event in which he participated, including his many years as a participant at the Paris Salons, as follows: #102. *surtout lumineux, crystal et argenterie, pondeterie*; #104 *Cycas revolute. Coupe lumineux grave*; #105 *Horizons lorraine. Coupe luminaire*; #106 *Fleurs de palmier austral. Lampe, appliqué et lustre ivoire et cristaux montée*; #107 *Le Souvenir. Veilleuse en émaux gravés* (collection M. Houot). [# 102 Especially bright, crystal and silverware Pondeteria; # 104. Cycas revolute. Etched glass; # 105 Scenes of Lorraine. Cut glass; # 106 Flowers of the 'austral' palm. Wall lamp and chandelier mounted with ivory and crystals; # 107 The souvenir. Night light in etched enamel (collection M. Houot)]

Opposite Page.
Bottom left: The Dreyfus table lamp, c. 1898-1900, inscribed *La Vérité s'allumera comme une lampe*. Collection Badisches Landesmuseum, Karlsruhe

Bottom right: *Cycas Revolute* (Sago palm) illuminated vase, given to the botanist Georges Le Monnier by his students in 1904. Engraved within the palm decoration is a quotation by Edgar Quinet, *L'âme vraie est sur le chemin/de toutes des vérites* (The true soul is on the path of all truth). Collection Musée de l'Ecole de Nancy

Exposition d'Art Décoratif de 1904, Nancy.
GALLÉ. — Vitrines et Surtout de Table.

Exposition d'Art Décoratif de 1904, Nancy.
GALLÉ. — Lit et Vitrines.

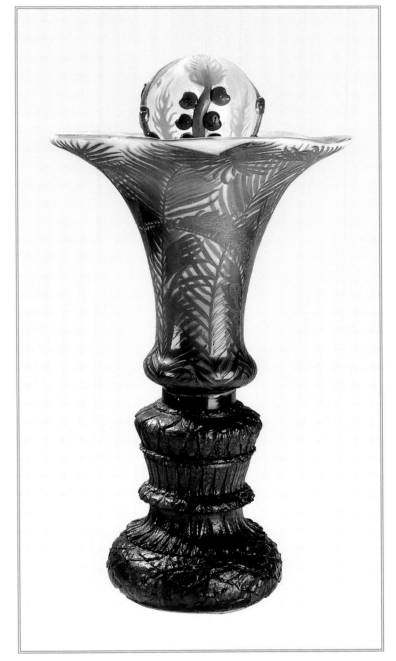

Exposition Internationale de l'Est de la France, Nancy, 1909

Three views of the Gallé display in the exhibition staged in the pavilion designed by Eugène Vallin in the Parc Sainte-Marie, Nancy, 1909, for current members of the Ecole de Nancy. Included in his honour was a retrospective ensemble of Gallé's furnishings lent by his widow, Henriette, in which several important light fixtures are visible.

View of the Exposition pavilion designed by Eugène Vallin. Illustrated in *Art et Industrie*, July 1909 (unpaginated).

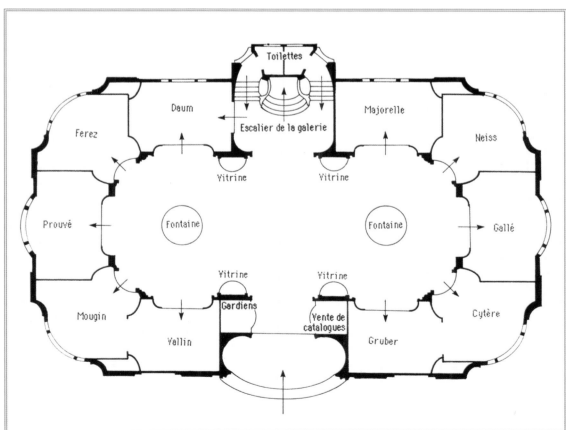

Layout of the exhibits, including those for Grüber, Vallin, Mougin, Majorelle, Daum, Ferez, Prouvé, Neiss and Cytère. The Gallé display is on the right.

Chapter 6:

IMAGE GALLERY

Small Domed / Conical Table Lamps

Plate 6.1.

Plate 6.2.

Plate 6.3.

Plate 6.4.

Plate 6.5.

Plate 6.6.

Plate 6.7.

Plate 6.8.

Plate 6.9.

Plate 6.10.

Plate 6.11.

Plate 6.12.

Plate 6.13.

Plate 6.14.

Plate 6.15.

Plate 6.16.

Plate 6.17.

Plate 6.18.

Plate 6.19.

Plate 6.20.

Plate 6.21.

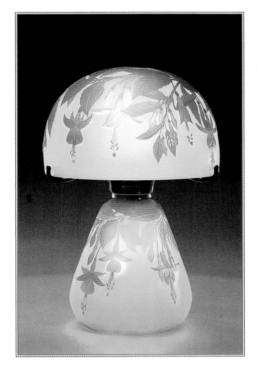

Plate 6.22.

Plate 6.23.

Plate 6.24.

Plate 6.25.

Plate 6.26.

Plate 6.27.

Plate 6.28.

Plate 6.29.

Plate 6.30.

Plate 6.31.

Plate 6.32.

Plate 6.33.

Plate 6.34.

Plate 6.35.

Plate 6.36.

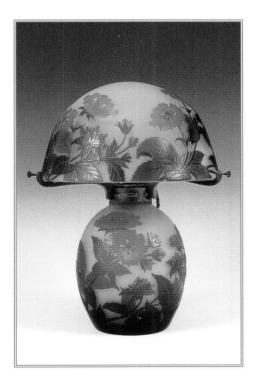

Plate 6.37.

Plate 6.38.

Plate 6.39.

Plate 6.40.

Plate 6.41.

Plate 6.42.

Plate 6.43.

Plate 6.44.

Plate 6.45.

Plate 6.46.

Plate 6.47.

Plate 6.48.

Plate 6.49.

Plate 6.50.

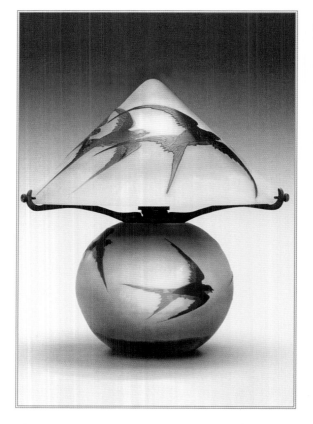

Plate 6.51.

Plate 6.52.

Plate 6.53.

Plate 6.54.

Plate 6.55.

Plate 6.56.

Plate 6.57.

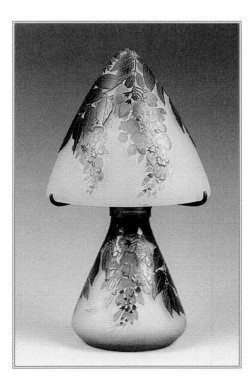

Plate 6.58.

Plate 6.59.

Plate 6.60.

Plate 6.61.

Plate 6.62.

Plate 6.63.

Plate 6.64.

Plate 6.65.

Plate 6.66.

Plate 6.67.

Plate 6.68.

Plate 6.69.

Plate 6.70.

Plate 6.71.

Plate 6.72.

Plate 6.73.

Plate 6.74.

Plate 6.75.

Plate 6.76.

Plate 6.77.

Plate 6.78.

Plate 6.79.

Plate 6.80.

Plate 6.81.

Plate 6.82.

Plate 6.83.

Plate 6.84.

Plate 6.85.

Plate 6.86.

Plate 6.87.

Plate 6.88.

Plate 6.89.

TABLE LAMPS

Plate 7.1.

Plate 7.2.

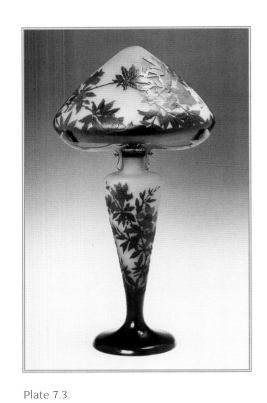

Plate 7.3.

Plate 7.4.

Plate 7.5.

Plate 7.6.

Plate 7.7.

Plate 7.8.

Plate 7.9.

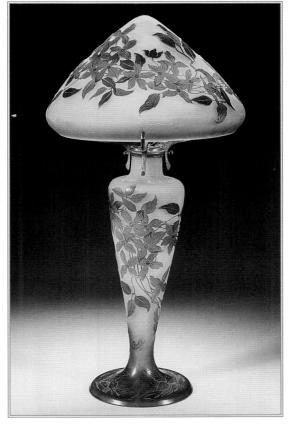

Plate 7.10.

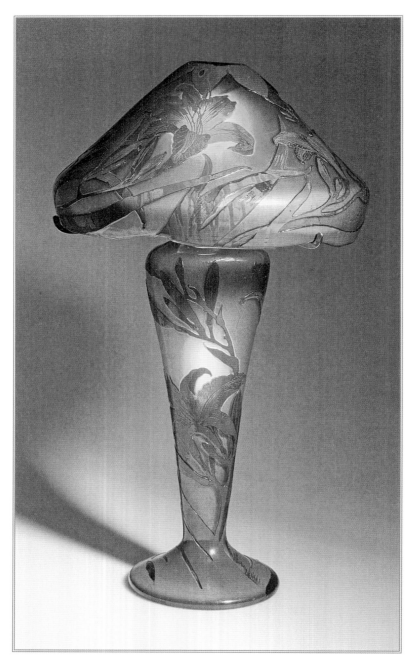

Plate 7.11.

Plate 7.12.

Plate 7.13.

Plate 7.14.

Plate 7.15.

Plate 7.16.

Plate 7.17.

Plate 7.18.

Plate 7.19.

Plate 7.20.

Plate 7.21.

Plate 7.22.

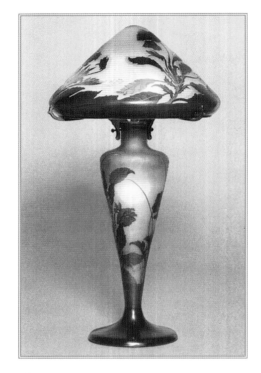

Plate 7.23.

Plate 7.24.

Plate 7.25.

Plate 7.26.

Plate 7.27. (Base attributed to Peter Tereszuk)

Plate 7.28.

Plate 7.29.

Plate 7.30.

Plate 7.31.

Plate 7.32.

Plate 7.33.

Plate 7.34.

Plate 7.35.

Plate 7.36.

Plate 7.37.

Plate 7.38.

Plate 7.39.

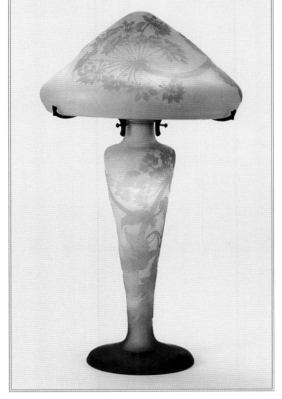

Plate 7.40.

Plate 7.41.

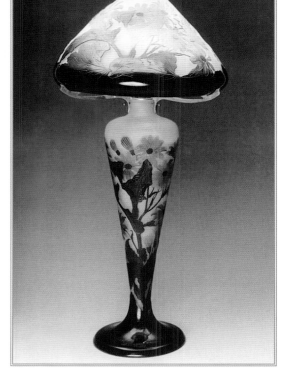

Plate 7.42.

Plate 7.43.

Plate 7.44.

Plate 7.45.

Plate 7.46.

Plate 7.47.

Plate 7.48.

Plate 7.49.

Plate 7.50.

Plate 7.51.

Plate 7.52.

Plate 7.53.

Plate 7.54.

Plate 7.55.

Plate 7.56.

Plate 7.57.

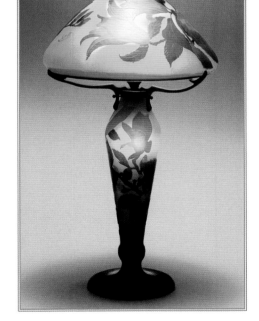

Plate 7.58.

Plate 7.59.

Plate 7.60.

Plate 7.61.

Plate 7.62.

Plate 7.63.

Plate 7.64.

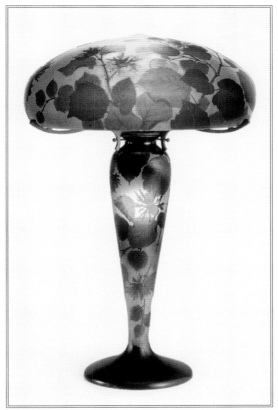

Plate 7.65.

Plate 7.66.

Plate 7.67.

Plate 7.68.

Plate 7.69.

Plate 7.70.

Plate 7.71.

Plate 7.72.

Plate 7.73.

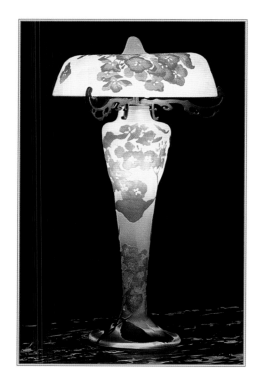

Plate 7.74.

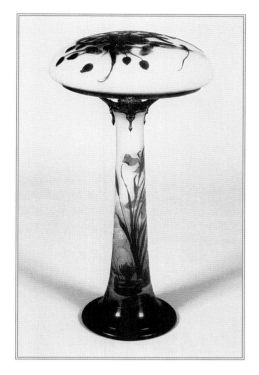

Plate 7.75.

Plate 7.76.

Plate 7.77.

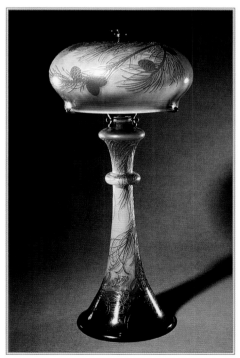

Plate 7.78.

Plate 7.79.

Plate 7.80.

Plate 7.81.

Plate 7.82.

Plate 7.83.

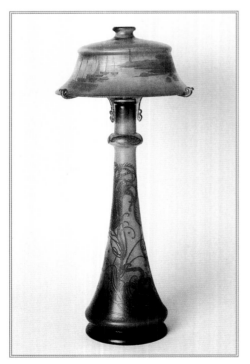

Plate 7.84.

Plate 7.85.

Plate 7.86.

Plate 7.87.

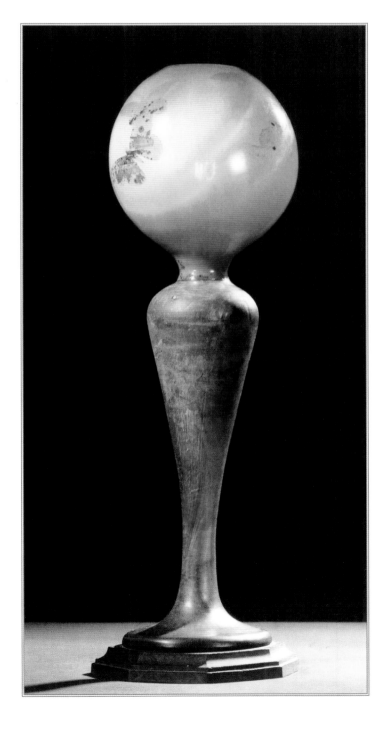

Plate 7.88.

Plate 7.89.

Plate 7.90.

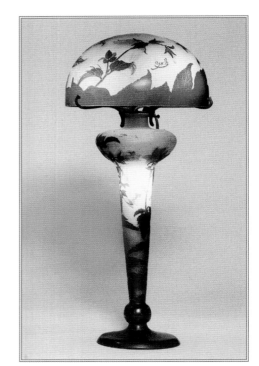

Plate 7.91.

Plate 7.92.

Plate 7.93.

Plate 7.94.

Plate 7.95.

Plate 7.96.

Plate 7.97.

Plate 7.98.

Plate 7.99.

Plate 7.100.

Plate 7.101.

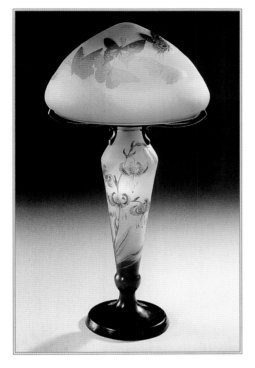

Plate 7.102.

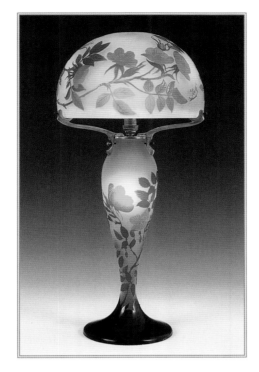

Plate 7.103.

Plate 7.104.

Plate 7.105.

Plate 7.106.

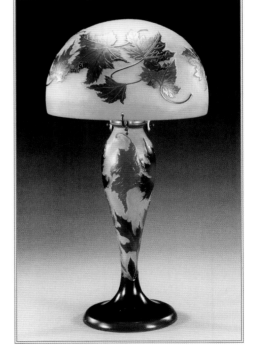

Plate 7.107.

Plate 7.108.

Plate 7.109.

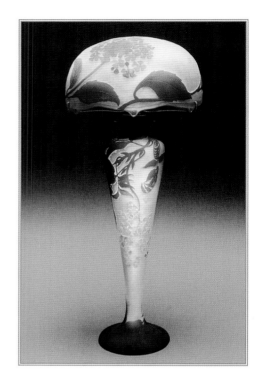

Plate 7.110.

Plate 7.111.

Plate 7.112.

Plate 7.113.

Plate 7.114.

Plate 7.115.

Plate 7.116.

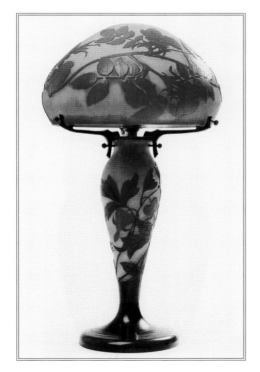

Plate 7.117.

Plate 7.118.

Plate 7.119.

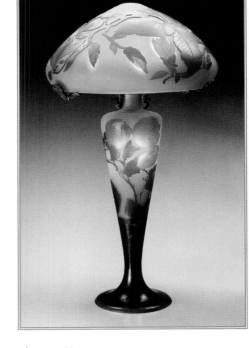

Plate 7.120.

Plate 7.121.

Plate 7.122.

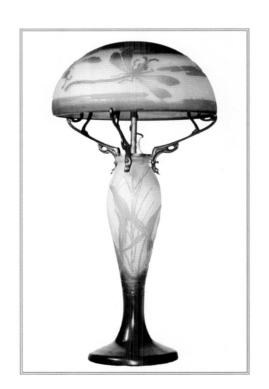

Plate 7.123.

Plate 7.124.

Plate 7.125.

Plate 7.126.

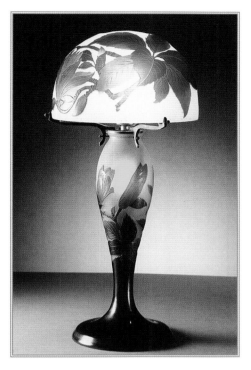

Plate 7.127.

Plate 7.128.

Plate 7.129.

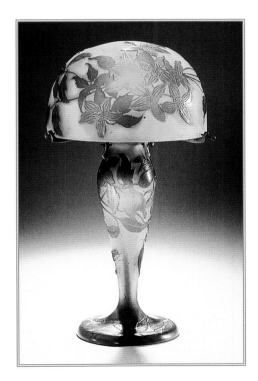

Plate 7.130.

Plate 7.131.

Plate 7.132.

Plate 7.133.

Plate 7.134.

Plate 7.135.

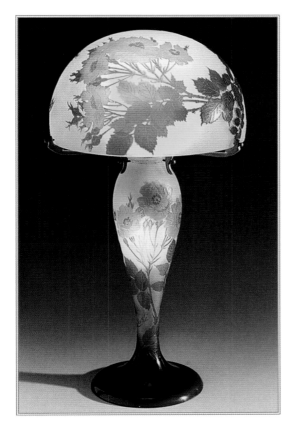

Plate 7.136.

Plate 7.137.

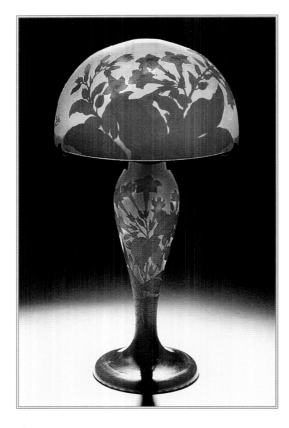

Plate 7.138.

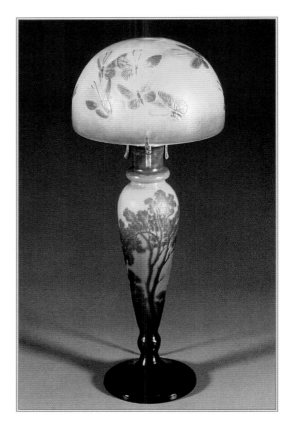

Plate 7.139.

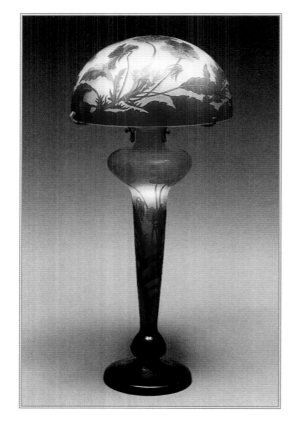

Plate 7.140.

Plate 7.141.

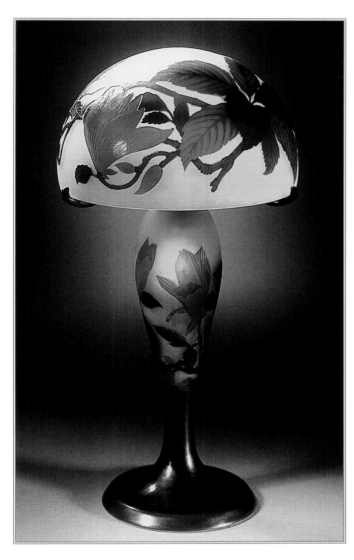

Plate 7.142.

Plate 7.143.

Plate 7.144.

Plate 7.145.

Plate 7.146.

Plate 7.147.

Plate 7.148.

Plate 7.149.

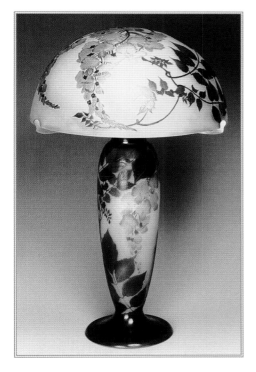

Plate 7.150.

Plate 7.151.

Plate 7.152.

Plate 7.153.

Plate 7.154.

Plate 7.155.

Plate 7.156.

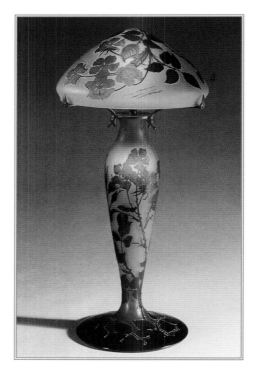

Plate 7.157.

Plate 7.158.

Plate 7.159.

Plate 7.160.

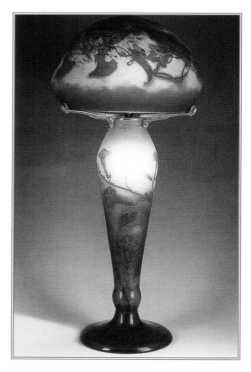

Plate 7.161.

Plate 7.162.

Plate 7.163.

Plate 7.164.

Plate 7.165.

Plate 7.166.

Plate 7.167.

Plate 7.168.

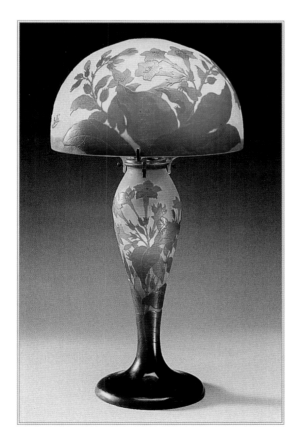

Plate 7.169.

Plate 7.170.

Plate 7.171.

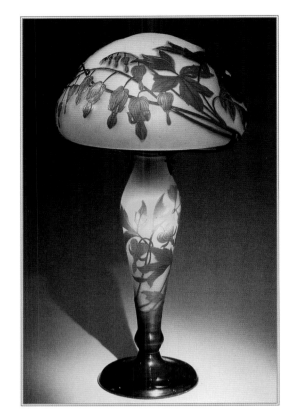

Plate 7.172.

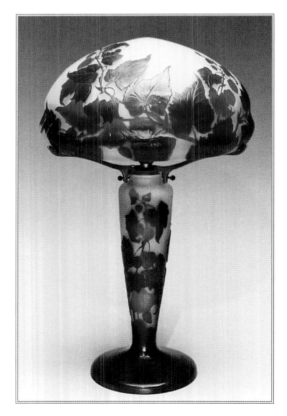

Plate 7.173.

Plate 7.174.

Plate 7.175.

Plate 7.176.

Plate 7.177.

Plate 7.178.

Plate 7.179.

Plate 7.180.

Plate 7.181.

Plate 7.182.

Plate 7.183.

Plate 7.184.

Plate 7.185.

Plate 7.186.

Plate 7.187.

Plate 7.188.

Plate 7.189.

Plate 7.190.

Plate 7.191.

Plate 7.192.

Plate 7.193.

Plate 7.194.

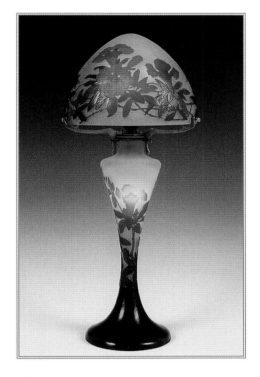

Plate 7.195.

Plate 7.196.

Plate 7.197.

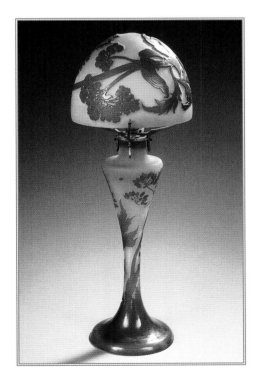

Plate 7.198.

Plate 7.199.

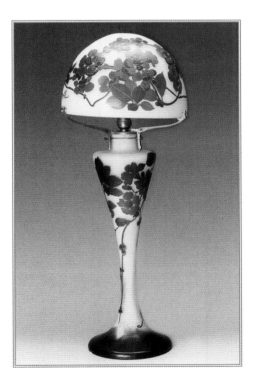

Plate 7.200.

Plate 7.201.

Plate 7.202.

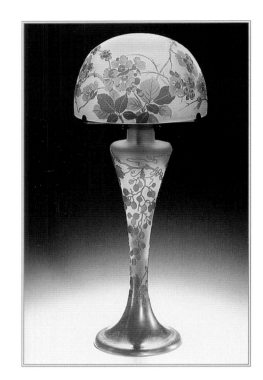

Plate 7.203.

Plate 7.204.

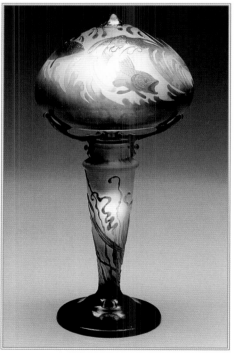

Plate 7.205.

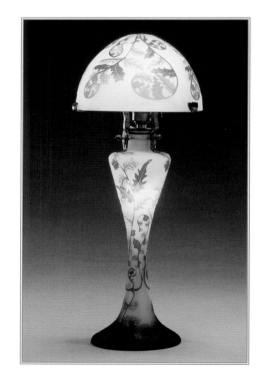

Plate 7.206.

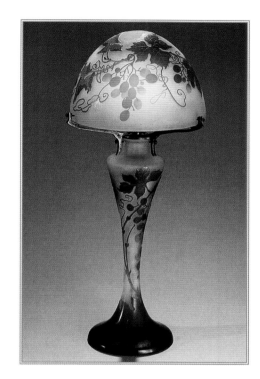

Plate 7.207.

Plate 7.208.

Plate 7.209.

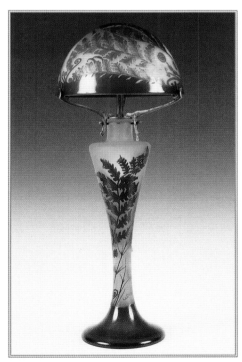

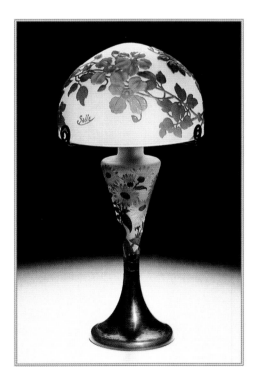

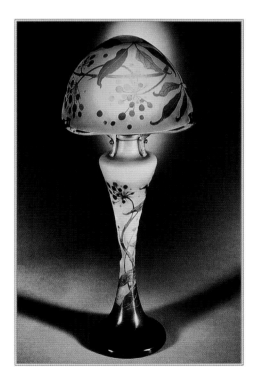

Plate 7.210.

Plate 7.211.

Plate 7.212.

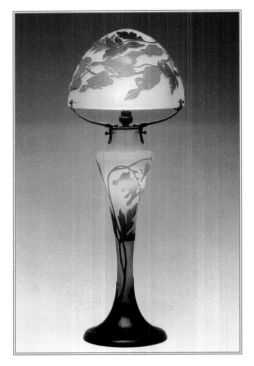

Plate 7.213.

Plate 7.214.

Plate 7.215.

Plate 7.216.

Plate 7.217.

Plate 7.218.

Plate 7.219.

Plate 7.220.

Plate 7.221.

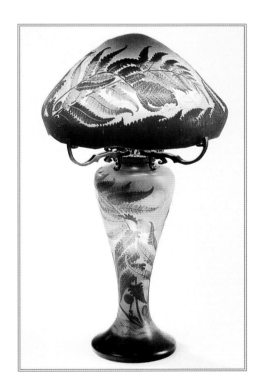

Plate 7.222.

Plate 7.223.

Plate 7.224.

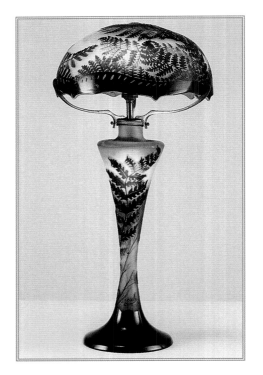

Plate 7.225.

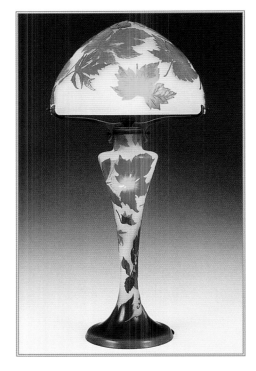

Plate 7.226.

Plate 7.227.

Plate 7.228.

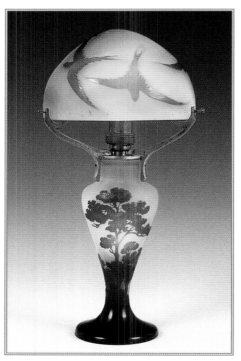

Plate 7.229.

Plate 7.230.

Plate 7.231.

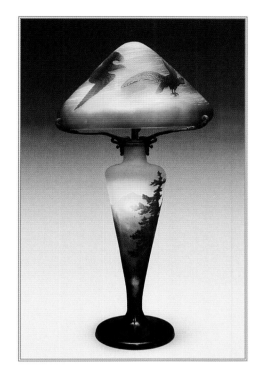

Plate 7.232.

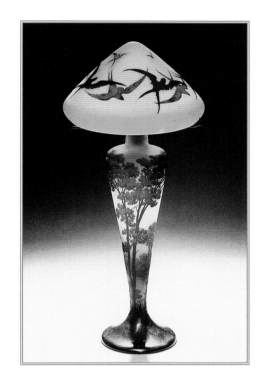

Plate 7.233.

Plate 7.234.

Plate 7.235.

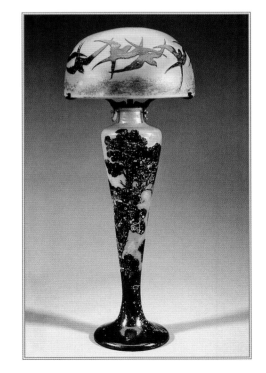

Plate 7.236.

Plate 7.237.

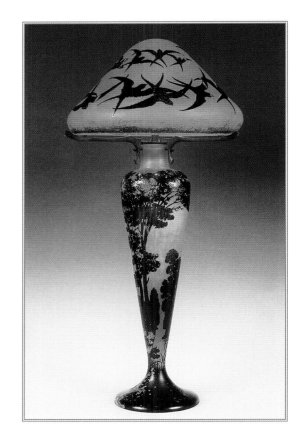

Plate 7.238.

Plate 7.239.

Plate 7.240.

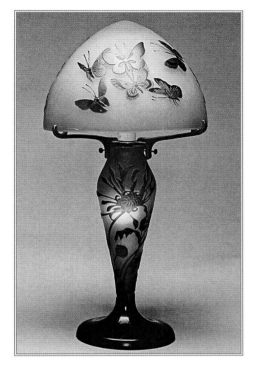

Plate 7.241.

Plate 7.242.

Plate 7.243.

Plate 7.244.

Plate 7.245.

Plate 7.246.

Plate 7.247.

Plate 7.248.

Plate 7.249.

Plate 7.250.

Plate 7.251.

Plate 7.252.

Plate 7.253.

Plate 7.254.

Plate 7.255.

Plate 7.256.

Plate 7.257.

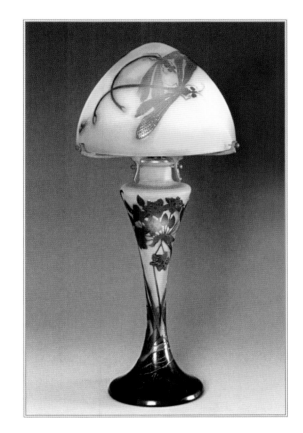

Plate 7.258.

Plate 7.259.

Plate 7.260.

Plate 7.261.

Plate 7.262.

Plate 7.263.

Plate 7.264.

Plate 7.265.

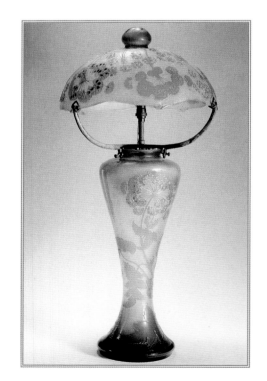

Plate 7.266.

Plate 7.267.

Plate 7.268.

Plate 7.269.

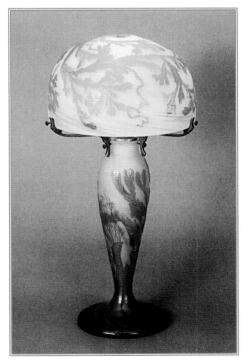

Plate 7.270.

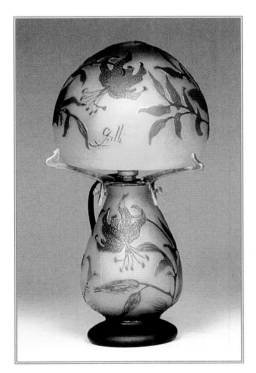

Plate 7.271.

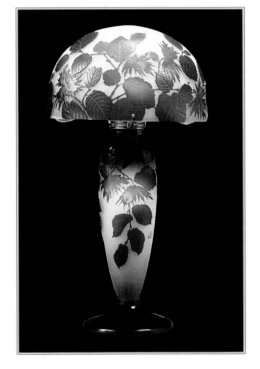

Plate 7.272.

Plate 7.273.

Plate 7.274.

Plate 7.275.

Plate 7.276.

Plate 7.277.

Plate 7.278.

Plate 7.279.

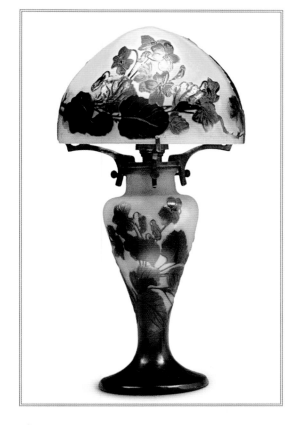

Plate 7.280.

Plate 7.281.

Plate 7.282.

Plate 7.283.

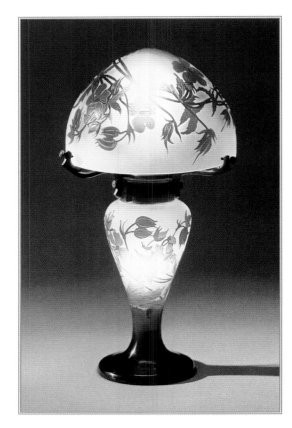

Plate 7.284.

Plate 7.285.

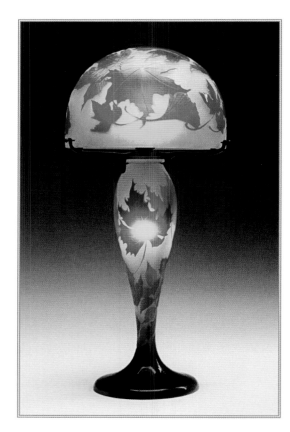

Plate 7.286.

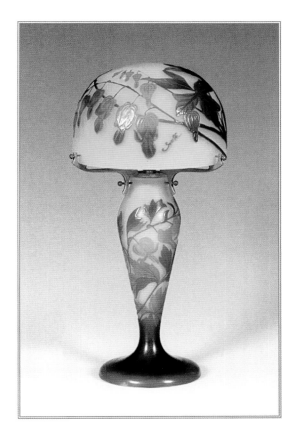

Plate 7.287.

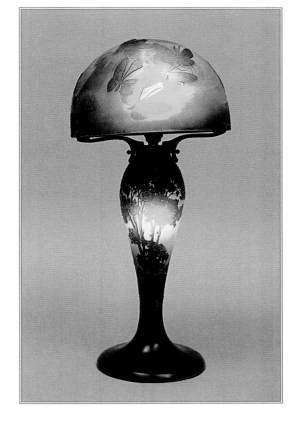

Plate 7.288.

Plate 7.289.

Plate 7.290.

Plate 7.291.

Plate 7.292.

Plate 7.293.

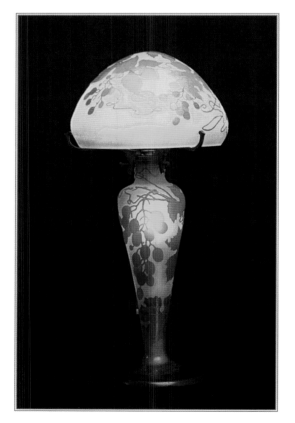

Plate 7.294.

Plate 7.295.

Plate 7.296.

Plate 7.297.

Plate 7.298.

Plate 7.299.

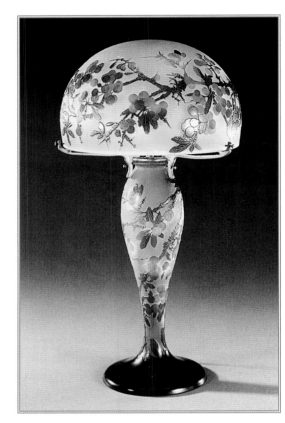

Plate 7.300.

Plate 7.301.

Plate 7.302.

Plate 7.303.

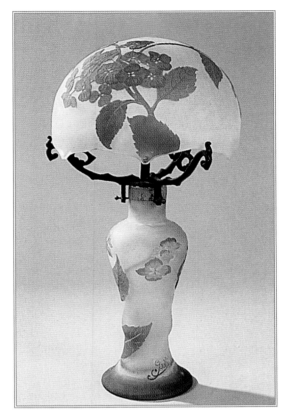

Plate 7.304.

Plate 7.305.

Plate 7.306.

Plate 7.307.

Plate 7.308.

Plate 7.309.

Plate 7.310.

Plate 7.311.

Plate 7.312.

Plate 7.313.

Plate 7.314.

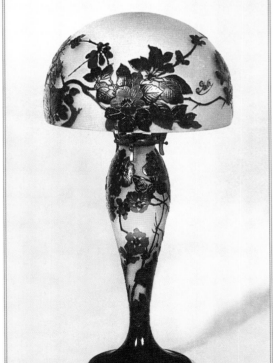

Plate 7.315.

Plate 7.316.

Plate 7.317.

Plate 7.318.

Plate 7.319.

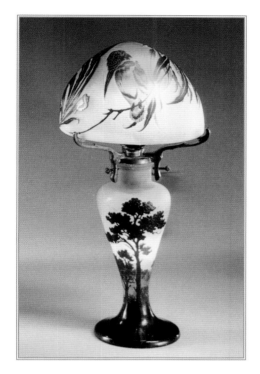

Plate 7.320.

Plate 7.321.

Plate 7.322.

Plate 7.323.

Plate 7.324.

Plate 7.325.

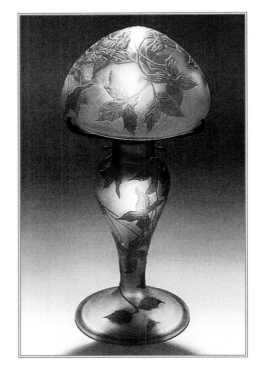

Plate 7.326.

Plate 7.327.

Plate 7.328.

Plate 7.329.

Plate 7.330.

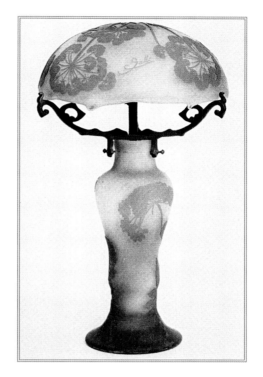

Plate 7.331.

Plate 7.332.

Plate 7.333.

Plate 7.334.

Plate 7.335.

Plate 7.336.

Veilleuses (Night Lights)

Plate 8.1.

Plate 8.2.

Plate 8.3.

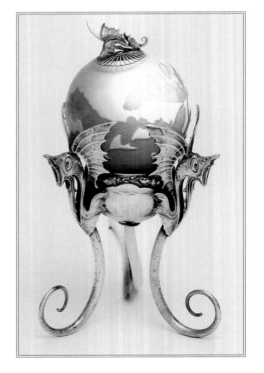

Plate 8.4.

Plate 8.5.

Plate 8.6.

Plate 8.7.

Plate 8.8.

Plate 8.9.

Plate 8.10.

Plate 8.11.

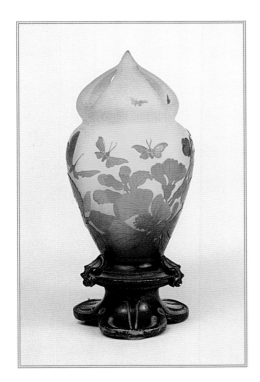

Plate 8.12.

Plate 8.13.

Plate 8.14.

Plate 8.15.

Plate 8.16.

Plate 8.17.

Plate 8.18.

CEILING FIXTURES

Plate 9.1.

Plate 9.2.

Plate 9.3.

Plate 9.4.

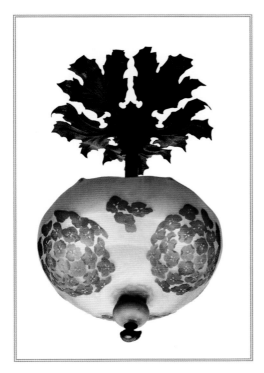

Plate 9.5.

Plate 9.6.

Plate 9.7.

Plate 9.8.

Plate 9.9.

Plate 9.10.

Plate 9.11.

Plate 9.12.

Plate 9.13.

Plate 9.14.

Plate 9.15.

Plate 9.16.

Plate 9.17.

Plate 9.18.

Plate 9.19.

Plate 9.20.

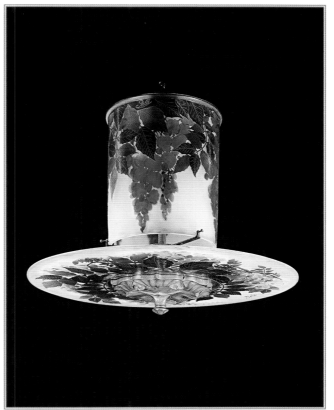

Plate 9.21.

Plate 9.22.

Plate 9.23.

Plate 9.24.

Plate 9.25.

Plate 9.26.

Plate 9.27.

Plate 9.28.

Plate 9.29.

Plate 9.30.

Plate 9.31.

Plate 9.32.

Plate 9.33.

Plate 9.34.

Plate 9.35.

Plate 9.36.

Plate 9.37.

Plate 9.38.

Plate 9.39.

Plate 9.40.

Plate 9.41.

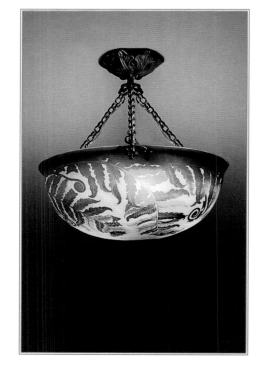

Plate 9.42.

Plate 9.43.

Plate 9.44.

Plate 9.45.

Plate 9.46.

Plate 9.47.

Plate 9.48.

Plate 9.49.

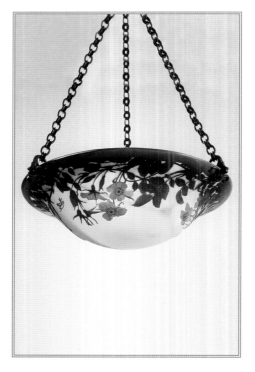

Plate 9.50.

Plate 9.51.

Plate 9.52.

Plate 9.53.

Plate 9.54.

Plate 9.55.

Plate 9.56.

Plate 9.57.

Plate 9.58.

Plate 9.59.

Plate 9.60.

Plate 9.61.

Plate 9.62.

Plate 9.63.

Plate 9.64.

Plate 9.65.

Plate 9.66.

Plate 9.67.

Plate 9.68.

Plate 9.69.

Plate 9.70.

Plate 9.71.

Plate 9.72.

Plate 9.73.

Plate 9.74.

Plate 9.75.

Plate 9.76.

Plate 9.77.

Plate 9.78.

Plate 9.79.

Plate 9.80.

Plate 9.81.

Plate 9.82.

Plate 9.83.

Plate 9.84.

Plate 9.85.

Plate 9.86.

Plate 9.87.

Plate 9.88.

Plate 9.89.

Plate 9.90.

Plate 9.91.

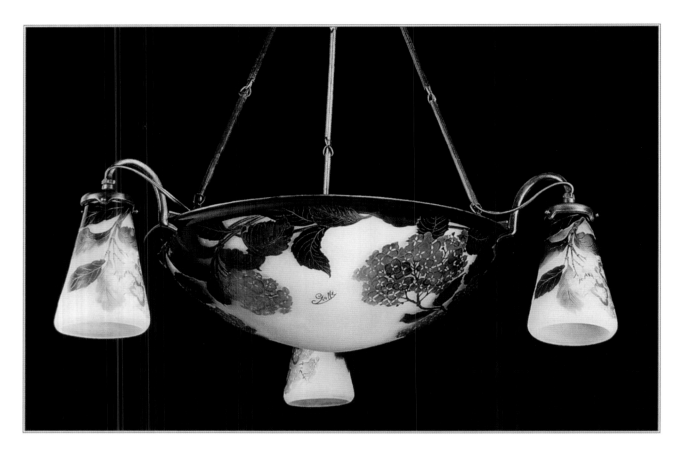

Plate 9.92.

Plate 9.93.

Plate 9.94.

Plate 9.95.

Plate 9.96.

Plate 9.97.

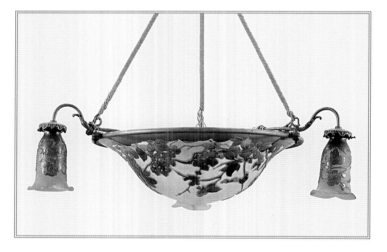

Plate 9.98.

Plate 9.99.

Plate 9.100.

Plate 9.101.

Plate 9.102.

Plate 9.103.

Plate 9.104.

Plate 9.105.

Plate 9.106.

Plate 9.107.

Plate 9.108.

Plate 9.109.

Plate 9.110.

Plate 9.111.

Plate 9.112.

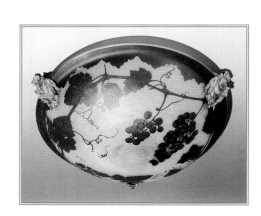

Plate 9.113.

Plate 9.114.

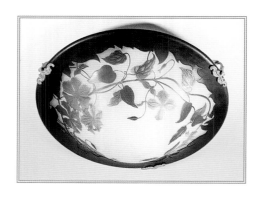

Plate 9.115.

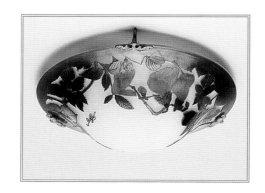

Plate 9.116.

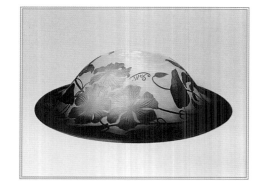

Plate 9.117.

Plate 9.118.

Plate 9.119.

Plate 9.120.

Plate 9.121.

Plate 9.122.

Plate 9.123.

Plate 9.124.

Plate 9.125.

Plate 9.126.

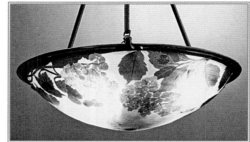

Plate 9.127.

Plate 9.128.

Plate 9.129.

Plate 9.130.

Plate 9.131.

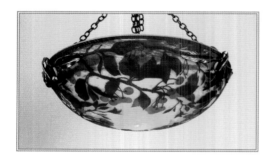

Plate 9.132.

Plate 9.133.

Plate 9.134.

Plate 9.135.

Plate 9.136.

Plate 9.137.

Plate 9.138.

Plate 9.139.

Plate 9.140.

Plate 9.141.

Plate 9.142.

Plate 9.143.

Plate 9.144.

Plate 9.145.

Plate 9.146.

Plate 9.147.

Plate 9.148.

Plate 9.149.

Plate 9.150.

Plate 9.151.

Plate 9.152.

Plate 9.153.

Plate 9.154.

Plate 9.155.

Plate 9.156.

Plate 9.157.

Plate 9.158.

Plate 9.159.

Plate 9.160.

Plate 9.161.

Plate 9.162.

Plate 9.163.

Plate 9.164.

Plate 9.165.

Plate 9.166.

Plate 9.167.

Plate 9.168.

Plate 9.169.

Plate 9.170.

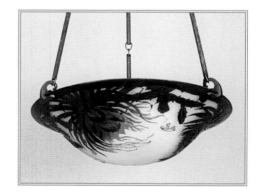

Plate 9.171.

Plate 9.172.

Plate 9.173.

Plate 9.174.

Plate 9.175.

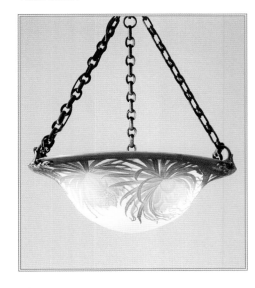

Plate 9.176.

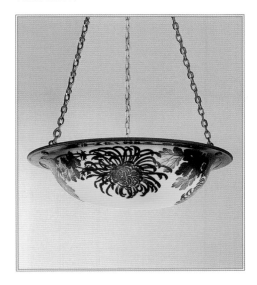

Plate 9.177.

Plate 9.178.

Plate 9.179.

Plate 9.180.

Plate 9.181.

Plate 9.182.

Plate 9.183.

Plate 9.184.

Plate 9.185.

Plate 9.186.

Plate 9.187.

Plate 9.188.

Plate 9.189.

Plate 9.190.

Plate 9.191.

Plate 9.192.

Plate 9.193.

Plate 9.194.

Plate 9.195.

Plate 9.196.

Plate 9.197.

Plate 9.198.

Plate 9.199.

Plate 9.200.

Plate 9.201.

Plate 9.202.

Plate 9.203.

Plate 9.204.

Plate 9.205.

Plate 9.206.

Plate 9.207.

Plate 9.208.

Plate 9.209.

Plate 9.210.

Plate 9.211.

Plate 9.212.

Wall Sconces

Plate 10.1.

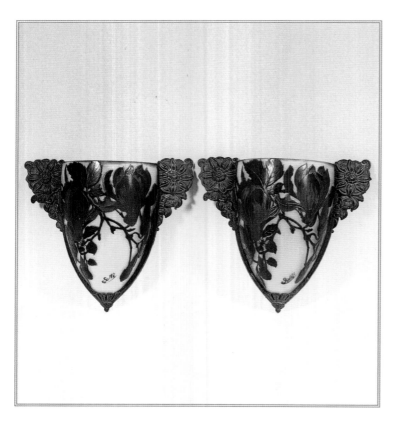

Plate 10.2.

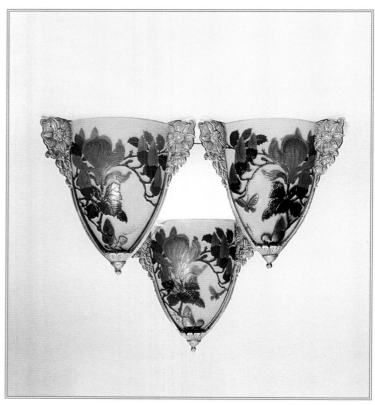

Plate 10.3.

Plate 10.4.

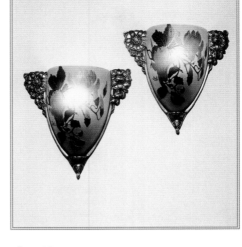

Plate 10.5.

Plate 10.6.

Plate 10.7.

Plate 10.8.

Plate 10.9.

Plate 10.10.

Plate 10.11.

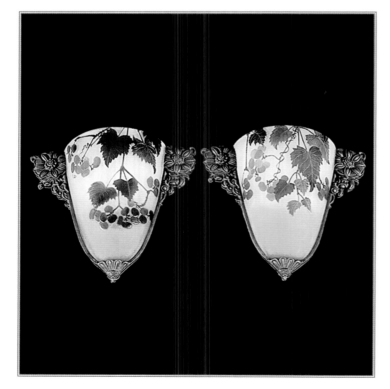

Plate 10.12.

Plate 10.13.

Plate 10.14.

Plate 10.15.

Plate 10.16.

Plate 10.17.

Plate 10.18.

Plate 10.19.

Plate 10.20.

Plate 10.21.

Plate 10.22.

Plate 10.23.

Plate 10.24.

Plate 10.25.

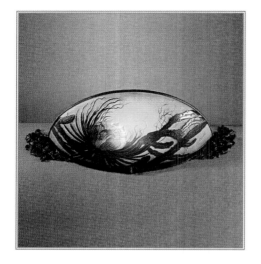

Plate 10.26.

Plate 10.27.

Plate 10.28.

Plate 10.29.

Plate 10.30.

Plate 10.31.

Plate 10.32.

Plate 10.33.

Plate 10.34.

Plate 10.35.

BIBLIOGRAPHY

Babin, Gustave, "Emile Gallé", L'Illustration, 1 October, 1904, #3214,

Barrelet, James, La Verrerie en France, Paris, 1953

Bénédite, Léonce, "Exposition internationale de 1900 à Paris", Rapports du jury international. Introduction generale, t. I, 2e partie, Paris, 1902

Bloch-Dermant, Janine, The Art of French Glass, 1860-1914, London, 1980

Bossaglia, Rossana, Art Nouveau, 1981

Champier, Victor "Les cadeaux offerts a l'escadre russe", Revue des Arts décoratifs, November, 1893

Charpentier, Françoise-Thérèse, "L'Ecole de Nancy", Jardin des Arts, November, 1960

Charpentier, Françoise-Thérèse, "L'Art de Gallé a-t-il ete influence par Baudelaire?", Gazette des Beaux-Arts, June, 1963

Charpentier, Françoise-Thérèse, "Emile Gallé", Université de Nancy II, Nancy, 1978

Promenades aux Salons. II. Emile Gallé, ébèniste et verrier", Le Journal des Debats, 13 May, 1893

De Bartha, Georges, L'Art 1900. La Collection Neumann, 1990

Debize, Christian, "Emile Gallé and the 'école de Nancy'", 1999

"Exposition Lorraine. L'Ecole de Nancy au Musée de l'Union centrale des Arts Décoratifs", 1ere serie: Le Mobilier; 2e serie: Objets d'art, verrerie; Ceramique, Cuir d'Art, Bronzes, Paris, 1903

Duncan, Alastair, Art Nouveau and Art Deco Lighting, London, 1978

Duncan, Alastair and De Bartha, Georges, Glass by Gallé, London, 1984

Fourcaud, Louis de, "L'Exposition universelle. Le Bois", La Revue de l'Art ancien et moderne, December, 1900

Fourcaud, Louis de, Emile Gallé, Paris, 1903

Frantz, Henri, "Art at Nancy Emile Gallé", The Magazine of Art, 1897

Gallé, Emile, "Mes envois au Salon", Revue des Arts Decoratifs, May, 1898

Gallé, Emile, "Les Fruits de l'Esprit", La Foi et la Vie, 15 April, 1899

Gallé, Emile, "Le Décor symbolique, discourse de reception a l'Academie de Stanislas, séance publique du 17 Mai, 1900", Nancy, 1900

Gallé, Emile, "Guide de l'envoi de Galle a l'exposition de 1900"

Gallé, Emile, "Ecrits pour l'art 1884-1889", Paris, 1908, and Laffitte Reprints, Marseille, 1980

Garner, Philippe, Emile Gallé, 1976

Henrivaux, Jules, "Emile Gallé", L'Art décoratif, January–June, 1905

Hofmann, Helga D., "Emile Gallé und Louis Majorelle – unbekannte Artbeiten und stilistiche Bemerkungen. Ein Beitrag zur "Ecole de Nancy", Kunst in Hessen und am Mittelrhein, 1968, no. 8

Jourdain, Francis, "Le Mobilier au salon nationale des Beaux-Arts", L'Art Décoratif, Janvier, 1903

Leroy, Maxime, "L'Ecole de Nancy au pavillon de Marsan", L'Art Décoratif, January, 1903

Marx, Roger, "La Lorraine a la Russie", La Revue Encyclopedique, 1 November, 1893, col. 635-640

Marx, Roger, "Les arts décoratifs (1893-1894)", La Revue Encyclopedique, 15 February, 1894

Marx, Roger, "E. Gallé psychologie de l'artiste et synthese de l'oeuvre", Art et Décoration, XXX, July-December, 1911

Marx, Roger, "L'Ecole de Nancy au Pavillon de Marsan", La Chronique des Arts et de la Curiosité, 14 March, 1893

Marx, Roger, "La Décoration et l'Art Industriel a l'exposition universelle de 1889", Ancienne Maison Quantin, Librairies – Imprimeries Reunies, 1890

Marx, Roger, "Emile Gallé, decorateur (1846-1904)", Revue Universelle, 15 November, 1904

Marx, Roger, "Emile Gallé", Art et Décoration, August, 1911

Marx, Roger, "Conference de M. Roger Marx sur Emile Gallé", Bulletin des Sociétés Artistiques de l'Est 1900-1904

Maus, Octave, "Necrologie. Emile Gallé", L'Art moderne, 2 October, 1904

Nicolas, Emile, "Emile Gallé a l'exposition de 1900", La Lorraine artiste, 15 October, 1900

Nicolas, Emile, "Emile Gallé", Le Pays Lorrain, 10 December, 1904

E.B., "Necrologie Emile Galle", Bulletin des Sociétés Artistiques de l'est 1900-1904

Anon., "L'Ecole de Nancy", La Revue Lorraine Illustrée, 1908

Rais, Jules, "L'Ecole de Nancy et son exposition au musée des arts décoratifs", Art et Décoration, January–June, 1903

Mme Sartor, Musée de Reims, "Catalogue sommaire de la collection Henry Vasnier, Reims", 1913

Saunier, Charles, "Les arts décoratifs aux Salons de 1902", Revue des Arts décoratifs, May, June, July 1902

Sedeyn, Emile, "Les arts décoratifs aux Salons de 1902. Société nationale des Beaux-Arts", L'Art décoratif, June, 1902

Thiebaut, Philippe, Emile Gallé, le magicien du verre, 2004

Varenne, Gaston, "Emile Gallé et l'école de Nancy", Pays lorraine, 1936

Verneuil, M. P., "L'Art decorative a la Société nationale", Art et Décoration, t. XIII, 1903

Magazines, Journals and Periodicals

Art et Industrie (Nancy), July, 1909, pp. 77-89; 1910, p. 79ff; January, 1911, p. 115

L'Art décoratif, July–Dec, 1901, p. 19; July–Dec 1902, pp. 169, 172; Jan 1903, pp. 176-177; 180, 212-214; Jan–June, 1905, pp. 97-98, 101-103, 111-112, 126-135, 259-260

Revue des Arts décoratifs, 1900, pp. 336-338; 1901, pp. 47, 374-375

La Lorraine artiste, 1899, pp. 5-7, 13-22, 60; 1900, pp. 98-100; 1901, pp. 25-30, 33-35, 59-60; 1903 pp. 83, 85, 215-216; 1904, pp. 37-40

Bulletin des Sociétés Artistiques de l'Est, 1900-1904, pp. 195-207

La Revue Lorraine Illustrée, No. 3, 1906, pp. 99, 129; 1908, p. 13

La Revue Lorraine Illustrée, 1903, p. 21

La Lorraine artiste

Le Bulletin des Sociétés industrielles de l'Est

The Magazine of Art, 1897/1898, p. 60

Revue de l'art ancien et moderne, 1902, pp. 344-345

La Revue des Arts Décoratifs (review of 1895 salon du Champ-de-Mars); 1901, p. 374

Emile Gallé 1900, exhibition catalogue, Exposition Universelle, Paris, 1900

Glasfax News Letter, Montreal, Canada, Vol. 8, No. 6, Sept 1974

"Gallé", exhibition catalogue, Musée du Luxembourg, 29 November 1985 – 2 February, 1986

"Exposition de l'alliance provinciale des industries d'art: école de Nancy", Pavillon de Marsan, Paris, March, 1903

"Nancy 1900", Rayonnement de l'art nouveau (Gerard Klopp, ed.), 1989

Art Nouveau L'Ecole de Nancy, Denoel et Serpenoise, 1987

"Cristallerie et ébénisterie d'art d'Emile Gallé, Etablissements GALLE", sales catalogue, Société anonyme, Nancy, 13 September, 1927

Anon., "L'Exposition d'art décoratif Lorrain a Nancy", Jan–June, 1905, pp. 97-127

Anon., "M. Emile Gallé a l'exposition", *La Lorraine*, 15 October, 1900, pp. 97ff

Art et industrie (Nancy), July, 1909

Exposition catalogue, Société Lorraine Amis des Arts, Nancy, 1904

Les Dessins de Gallé: Emile Gallé et ses Ateliers, Kyuryudo Publishing, Co., 1988

INDEX - GENERAL

Page numbers in **bold** refer to illustrations and/or captions

Index of Exhibitions and Expositions

Index of Gallé Designs